For an Amerindian Au
An Essay on the Foundations of a Social Ethic

Born and raised at Wendake Reserve near Quebec City, Sioui is proud to be a Huron and an Amerindian. He is fully aware of the injustices that the aboriginal people of North America have suffered – and continue to suffer – at the hands of Euroamericans. He is convinced that the greatness of Amerindians does not lie only in the past and that Native peoples will play an even more important role in the future by providing ideas essential to creating a viable way of life for North America and the world.

For An Amerindian Autohistory is a work not only of metahistory but of moral reflection. Georges Sioui contrasts Euroamerican ethnocentrism and feelings of racial superiority with the Amerindian belief in the "Great Circle of Life" and shows that human beings must establish intellectual and emotional connections with the entire living world if they hope to achieve abundance, equality, and peace for all.

While this is a polemical work, Sioui never descends to recrimination or vituperative condemnation, even when that might seem justified. Instead, he has given us a polemic that is written at the level of philosophy.

GEORGES E. SIOUI is associate professor, Department of Indian Studies, and dean of Academics, Saskatchewan Indian Federated College, University of Regina.

McGill-Queen's Native and Northern Series
Bruce G. Trigger, Editor

1 When the Whalers Were Up North
Inuit Memories from the Eastern Arctic
Dorothy Harley Eber

2 The Challenge of Arctic Shipping
Science, Environmental Assessment, and Human Values
David L. VanderZwaag and Cynthia Lamson, Editors

3 Lost Harvests
Prairie Indian Reserve Farmers and Government Policy
Sarah Carter

4 Native Liberty, Crown Sovereignty
The Existing Aboriginal Right of Self-Government in Canada
Bruce Clark

5 Unravelling the Franklin Mystery
Inuit Testimony
David C. Woodman

6 Otter Skins, Boston Ships, and China Goods
The Maritime Fur Trade of the Northwest Coast, 1785–1841
James R. Gibson

7 From Wooden Ploughs to Welfare
The Story of the Western Reserves
Helen Buckley

8 In Business for Ourselves
Northern Entrepreneurs
Wanda A. Wuttunee

9 For an Amerindian Autohistory
An Essay on the Foundations of a Social Ethic
Georges E. Sioui

For an Amerindian Autohistory

An Essay on the Foundations of a Social Ethic

GEORGES E. SIOUI

Translated from the French by
SHEILA FISCHMAN

Foreword by
BRUCE G. TRIGGER

McGill-Queen's University Press
Montreal & Kingston • London • Buffalo

ISBN 0-7735-0950-x (cloth)
ISBN 0-7735-1328-0 (paper)

Legal deposit fourth quarter 1992
Bibliothèque nationale du Québec

Printed in Canada on acid-free paper
First paperback edition 1995

This book is a translation of *Pour une auto-histoire amérindienne*, published by Les Presses de l'Université Laval, 1991. Translation and publication have been supported by the Canada Council.

Canadian Cataloguing in Publication Data

Sioui, Georges E., 1948-
For an Amerindian autohistory
McGill-Queen's native and northern series,
ISSN 1181-7453
Translation of: Pour une autohistoire amérindienne.
Includes bibliographical references.
ISBN 0-7735-0950-x (bnd)
ISBN 0-7735-1328-0 (pbk)
1. Indians of North America – Canada – Historiography. 2. Indians of North America – Canada – History. 3. Indians of North America – Canada – Philosophy. I. Title. II. Series.
E76.8.S5513 1992 971.00497 0072
C92-090386-x

This book was typeset by
Typo Litho Composition Inc.
in 10/12 Palatino.

To my mother, Eléonore,
my father, Georges-Albert,
my wife, Barbara,
our son, Miguel Paul Sastaretsi.

To all our ancestors who speak through us.

CONTENTS

FOREWORD

I have long expressed the desire that more Native people should become centrally involved in the work of anthropology and ethnohistory. It is therefore an honour as well as a great pleasure to be invited to write this foreword for Georges Sioui's *For an Amerindian Autohistory*. In this book, Sioui attempts for the first time to establish from an Amerindian, and more specifically from a Huron, point of view the guidelines that should govern the study of Native history. He maintains that these guidelines are also essential for the self-image and social ethics of Native people and should govern the relations between Native people and more recent immigrants to the Americas. Hence Sioui has produced a work not only of metahistory but also of moral reflections. He is proud to be a Huron and an Amerindian and fully aware of the injustices that his people – Huron and Amerindian – have suffered and continue to suffer at the hands of Euroamericans. Yet he is convinced that the greatness of Amerindians does not lie only in the past; in the future Native peoples will play an even more important role by providing the model for a viable way for North America and the world. While this is a polemical work, it never descends to recrimination and vituperative condemnation, even when that might seem justified. Instead it is a polemic written at the level of philosophy. Surely all works of philosophy are polemical by their very nature.

What is autohistory? It is Native history written in accordance with Amerindian values – which means largely by Native people, although Sioui, unlike some other Amerindians, does not rule out the possibility that useful work can be done by non-Natives who take the trouble to acquire a sound working knowledge of Native values and understanding. The ultimate aim of such history is to discover what is special about Native cultures and to understand the role that Native people have played and will continue to play in terms of world history. Sioui is convinced, as are many other Native people, that Amerindian values have influenced Euroamerican behaviour far more than Euroamericans have modified the cultural code of Amerindians. He also believes that studying the persistence of essential Amerindian values, rather than the investigation of cultural transformations, is what is of primary interest to Native people and of greatest importance for understanding their role in world history. Despite change, the vision has remained the same. It is not clear to what extent Sioui would agree with Calvin Martin and some other scholars that an historical consciousness is alien to traditional Amerindian thought, but he certainly does not accept their proposition that it is impossible to write histories of societies that did not willingly launch themselves into an historical trajectory. On the contrary, his ultimate aim is to define the Amerindian place in history.

Sioui believes that traditional history has helped to reinforce barriers of mistrust and incomprehension between Native people and the peoples who have more recently established themselves on American soil. The chief flaw that Sioui sees in Euroamerican historiography is that it has internalized the values of cultural evolutionism. He does not deny the reality of technological development, but objects strenuously to cultural evolutionism's commitment to the belief that all forms of social, intellectual, and moral elaboration are correlated with, and ultimately derived from, technological change. He also objects to the view that peoples who failed to participate in this development throughout human history are bound to become extinct as a result of contact with "more evolved" peoples. Sioui is, of course, correct that these views dominated European and Euroamerican thinking in the nineteenth century and served as an excuse for depriving Native peoples around the world of their freedom, possessions, and sometimes of their very existence. It is also true that cultural evolutionism continued to colour the views that a considerable number of historians had of Native people into the 1970s. Yet Sioui is not willing to espouse the cultural relativism with which the American anthropologist Franz Boas and his students challenged cultural evolutionism, beginning in the late nineteenth century. According to this doctrine, one culture cannot be evaluated in terms of another but each must be understood and assessed on its own terms. Sioui, on the contrary, is convinced that, in many crucial respects, the value systems of Amerindians are superior to, and more viable than, those of Euroamericans. He offers us a world-view that is as self-assured, self-contained, and insistent on dissolving all alienating barriers between human groups as was the rationalist philosophy of the European Enlightenment.

Sioui contrasts an underlying Euroamerican ethnocentrism and sense of racial superiority with an Amerindian belief in the universal interdependence of all things and in the need for human beings to do all that they can to interconnect intellectually and emotionally with the entire living world so as to create abundance, quality, and peace for all. The Indian sacred circle of life is contrasted with the Eurocentric evolutionary myth. He might also have noted that the sacred circle stands in opposition to the far older, and still more influential, biblically inspired belief that God gave human beings the right to use all living things for their own purposes. Sioui argues that, while Native beliefs lead to restraint, contentment, and the conservation of the natural world, Western beliefs lead to oppression, coercion, and the destruction of the environment. He also stresses reason and the curbing of emotional excesses as core features of the Amerindian value system.

Some anthropologists, such as Edmund Leach, have denied that it is possible or worthwhile to demonstrate, even for historically well-documented peoples, that specific social values have persisted over long periods. Sioui offers two compelling pieces of evidence in support of his opposing claims: the short-term one historical, the long-term one ecological. In the first instance, he argues persuasively that the Baron de Lahontan, whose picture of Amerindian values closely resembles his own, was the first European to leave a written record of having understood Amerindian cultures from a Native point of view. This accords with my own conviction that Native cultures were better understood by European traders and ordinary people who lived on a day-by-day basis among Amerindians than by the priests and administrators who tried, often vainly, to change their ways of life. It also demonstrates that the so-called myth of the noble savage was not an invention of the salons of Paris, as is often claimed. Lahontan was the intellectual heir of Montaigne and Lescarbot, but his understanding was based on much greater experience of Native life and greatly exceeded that of these men. Its authenticity is also attested by Lafitau and earlier Jesuit writers, who frequently confirm Lahontan in matters of fact, although their attitudes toward Native cultures were radically different from his.

The long-term argument is more circumstantial but no less persuasive. Native people have occupied North America for many thousands of years, while inflicting little, if any, irreversible damage on the environment. Yet after only a few hundred years Euroamericans have inflicted so much damage on the ecosystem and on their own society that it is unlikely that our present way of life and its accompanying value system can survive much longer. A growing awareness of ecological problems suggests that ideas which resemble the Indian circle of life may indeed have more survival value than the evolutionary concepts that have guided the industrial revolution and created the present world crisis. All of this suggests that Sioui is right when he argues that Amerindian values rather than Euroamerican ones may embody hope for the future of all humanity.

Yet what is the nature of these values? Is it that, as a result of the privations Amerindians have suffered under Euroamerican domination, they have preserved the sort of values that are common to all small-scale egalitarian societies? Sioui himself seems to suggest this when he states that Europeans once had spiritual gifts that were lost in the course of technological development. There is also evidence that similar losses occurred (although to a lesser degree) as indigenous hierarchical societies, in which power and coercion played major roles, developed among the Native peoples of Mexico and Peru. Or do all Amerindians possess values that are a common heritage from some ancient past? My own belief is that both factors are involved. At least some beliefs about the relationship between human beings and the cosmos may date as early as the first appearance of human beings in the Americas. In the northeastern part of North America, the active preservation of an egalitarian social organization and of ancient cosmological views had sustained societies that in most respects were the direct antitheses of the European ones that launched the invasion of America in the sixteenth and seventeenth centuries.

Sioui argues that, despite colonization and oppression, the essential spirit of Native societies remains intact. From the beginning, he maintains, Amerindians tried to teach Europeans their view of the world. The Metis nation of western Canada provides evidence of their early success. Today, as Euroamerican values become increasingly maladaptive, the possibility grows that Euroamericans as a whole will have to abandon their cherished myths and adopt a view of the world akin to that of the sacred circle of life. Sioui, like the Ojibwa scholar Winona LaDuke and many Native spiritual chiefs and holy men, sees the Amerindian world-view as the salvation of North America and the world. He also looks forward to the day when, in his father's words, "the Indians will be understood and cease to suffer." This explains why, in his efforts to realize this historical goal, Sioui is anxious to assuage the feelings of guilt that he believes continue to estrange Euroamericans from their Amerindian kinsfolk.

By providing a systematic philosophical formulation of the ideas shared by many Native people, Sioui is making an important contribution to the dialogue between Native people and Euroamerican intellectuals, whom he desires to unite (together with all people) within the sacred circle of life. His arguments provide a more comprehensive framework for understanding the nature of Amerindian philosophy than does the current debate about whether or not in past times Amerindians were "natural ecologists." Many Amerindians and Euroamerican ecologists eagerly maintain that they were, while other Euroamerican historians and anthropologists suggest that to a large extent these claims are tales invented to suit the mood of the present day.

The importance of Sioui's philosophical contribution is also greater than his specific historical application of his ideas. While his view of the relationship between Huron, Iroquois, and Europeans in the seventeenth century is significantly different from any other known to me, modern Euroamerican scholars differ radically among themselves in their interpretations of that era. Some see the fur trade as paramount, while others argue that European goods were of only incidental interest to Native people. Some treat European interventions as crucial for shaping the history of that period; others argue that longstanding Native relations were of primary importance; and still others try to steer between these two extremes. As a result, there can be no simple dichotomy between Amerindian and Euroamerican viewpoints because, to begin with, there is no single Euroamerican view. Under these conditions, the more viewpoints there are the better, provided that all concerned remember that the primary test of any historical interpretation is its ability to account for the broadest and most detailed array of historical evidence. While Sioui's interpretations reflect his particular vision of the world, they are by no means the only reflection of that vision; nor are they incapable of revision as new data become available.

Finally, Sioui rightly draws attention to the injustice of a confrontational relationship between Amerindians and Euroamericans that is centred on the adjudication of land claims and historical rights by Euroamerican legal systems. He calls for relations between Native people and Euroamericans to be based on mutual respect and self-determination for minority groups.

I will end this foreword by stressing the practical importance to all North Americans of securing the economic and political rights of Native peoples. It is hard for even the strongest value system to survive when people are deprived of their independent sources of livelihood and subjected to grinding poverty, domination, and racial discrimination. Today Native people are, economically and socially, the most deprived of Canada's peoples. Across much of northern Canada and in the hearts of big cities, unemployment is rampant among Native people. The result is a high rate of alcoholism, drug abuse, suicide, violence, marital breakdown, imprisonment, disease, and educational failure. While many continue to find security in their traditional beliefs, others give way to despair or turn their hatred against their Euroamerican oppressors. The economic and political problems that lie at the heart of this situation are clearly the result of five hundred years of injustice inflicted on Native people by Euroamericans, eager to possess and exploit the riches of this continent. It is the moral responsibility of those in control, and the Euroamerican voters who keep them in power, to play a leading role in redressing these injustices. Native people are more determined than ever to resist oppression. The choice for Euroamericans is therefore either to degrade themselves further by trying to suppress this struggle or to change their ways and seek to right the injustices of the past and present. Sioui's book provides some indication of the generous response that awaits Euroamericans if, in Sioui's terms, they learn to think and behave more like Amerindians.

Bruce G. Trigger
McGill University

ACKNOWLEDGMENTS

I am pleased to express my gratitude to my research director, Jacques Mathieu. He was always available to me, and had the perspicacity to choose as co-director Denys Delâge, who has become my brother. My friendship and respect are also due to François Trudel, my ethnohistory professor, whose openness and encouragement were often very valuable.

Few Amerindians have had the opportunity to see the history of their nation given detailed study by so distinguished a thinker as Bruce G. Trigger, whose help and support have been unfailing both in the publication of the original French book and in its translation into English.

I am grateful as well to Jacques Chouinard, director of Les Presses de l'Université Laval, whose interest in my work made possible the initial publication of this book in French. I also wish to acknowledge the contributions of Geneviève Laplante, who revised the French text, and Geneviève Saladin, who saw it through the publishing process at Les Presses de l'Université Laval.

In preparing this translation for publication, I have again incurred many debts. In addition to Bruce Trigger, I wish to thank particularly Le Secrétariat des Affaires Autochtones du Québec for a grant that enabled me to write a preliminary English translation; Sheila Fischman, for her care and meticulousness as a translator; Curtis Fahey, for his thorough and sensitive editing of the manuscript; and the staff of McGill-Queen's University Press.

INTRODUCTION

Sad and confused, I headed home from school, having just received my first lesson in Canadian history. At the age of six I was starting my third year of primary school: a child from an Indian reservation, whose family had a below-average income but a strong Amerindian consciousness and pride.

"Your ancestors," said the imposing mother superior who taught us history, "were savages with no knowledge of God. They were ignorant and cared nothing about their salvation." And then, with a sincerity that sometimes had her close to tears: "The king of France took pity on them and sent missionaries who tried to convert them, but your ancestors, the savages, killed those missionaries, who became the blessed Canadian martyrs. Now, thanks to God and His Church, you are civilized people. You must ask God's pardon every day for the sins of your ancestors, and thank Him for introducing you to the Catholic faith, for snatching you from the hands of the Devil who kept your ancestors in a life of idolatry, theft, lying, and cannibalism. Now get down on your knees, we're going to pray to the blessed Canadian martyrs."

The story will be familiar to most people who have grown up and lived in some part of the American continent. But what should be equally familiar, even banal – and is not – is the fact that very few Euroamericans, anywhere on the continent, have had the common decency to imagine how devastating such teaching has been to the development of generations of young minds, and thus on their chances of making a dignified contribution to the advancement of human society. Similarly, few Euroamericans, when faced with Amerindian social reality, feel any spontaneous responsibility to help. The average North American's inability to react responsibly and constructively to the social and economic condition of Natives is easily understood once you know how the history of the New World has been written by most of the non-Natives who have taken an interest in it.

American history as a whole has erected walls and dug chasms of mistrust and incomprehension between the descendants of the aboriginal race and the nations newly formed on American soil, with all the associated consequences: poverty, the cultural degeneration of minorities and the powerless, racial conflicts, guilt, and widespread social impoverishment. In my opinion, two ideas generally accepted by the dominant society – ideas that this book sets out to destroy – account for the impasse in American cross-cultural communication.

First is the belief in the superiority of European culture and morality, which has served as a foundation for the acquisition of other peoples' territories and resources. Its scientific name is the theory of social evolution, which puts forward, as a truth, the principle that those peoples who possess the most "advanced" technology and the "capacity of writing" are in the vanguard of the process of "evolution," and thus have the right, inherent to their culture, and the responsibility, to bring about the "development" of the "less advanced." I call this theory the evolution myth. The second idea, which hinges on the first, is that of the inevitable disappearance of the Amerindian, or the myth of the disappearance of the Native. Such annihilation was regarded as the logical and normal outcome of the shock that occurs between a highly "advanced" civilization and another – particularly that of the New World Natives – very "backward" one. As William Robertson wrote in his 1777 *History of America*, "It is in America that man shows himself in the most simple form in which he can be conceived to exist. We can see there, societies barely beginning to form and can observe the feelings and actions of men in the infancy of social living."[1]

THE SACRED CIRCLE OF LIFE

I intend to explain the system of values proper to Native American societies, with particular reference to those in northeastern North America, and to demonstrate the persistence of the ideological traits so defined. Put simply, the Amerindian genius, acknowledging as it does the universal interdependence of all beings, physical and spiritual, tries by every available means to establish intellectual and emotional contact between them, so as to guarantee them – for they are all "relatives" – abundance, equality, and, therefore, peace. This is the sacred circle of life, which is opposed to the evolutionist conception of the world wherein beings are unequal, and are often negated, jostled, and made obsolete by others who seem adapted to evolution.

AMERINDIAN AUTOHISTORY

I have often been struck by the great difficulties peoples of Native culture encounter when they try to sensitize outsiders to their traditional values. I have also wondered why there is such a lack of intercultural communication in our society (and the world) and, most of all, how a collective and individual desire for such communication can be created. I was still quite young when I realized that the way history is dispensed to young children – in the absence of many really suitable pedagogical tools – is one of the underlying reasons for the prejudices that keep people from respecting first themselves (for, as an instrument of power, history has cultivated feelings of guilt in people of certain cultures), and then one another (since dividing is the eternal prerequisite for conquering).

The roots of this historical discourse are in a thought system far more ancient than the European presence in America. In reality, on this continent and elsewhere it has simply followed a course laid down long ago by such monumental thinkers as Aristotle and Plato. I used to tell myself that not even an Amerindian version of American history could change it. But then one night in 1954, my father, echoing so many obscure Indian thinkers who have lived since "contact," told his eldest son, to console him and to preserve his pride and faith in his ancestors: "My son, if you want to succeed in school and later on in life, you must write down what you are told to be the truth; but don't believe that it is the truth. Our ancestors were good and generous, and they lived very happily here, on their land. Our people have suffered a great deal since the White people came here, though it's not the White people's fault. The Great Spirit wants them to be here and He wants us to help them. One day you will write other books about history, and help people to learn the truth. The day is coming when the Indians will be understood and cease to suffer. Time [as he often said] is the Father of Truth."

THE TWOFOLD AIM OF THIS BOOK

The goal of this book is first of all philosophical, since it sets out to demonstrate how the evolution myth can harm those who believe in it – and consequently, those who are victims of it – in their communications with people of other cultures, and how abandoning it in favour of the Native vision of the sacred circle of life may offer a timely alternative option to a modern society undergoing a crisis in values.

In an attempt to dispel the myth of the disappearance of the Native, this book also has a social function. For why should the governments of modern states adopt a policy for preserving cultural phenomena if Natives are officially extinct, or if their disappearance is imminent? What should political leaders do when the historical tradition responds to the desire of a "subculture" or "ethnic minority" to survive by advocating either commiseration, in the form of an always symbolic sum of money, or, worse, threats, punishment, suppression?

Within the same social design, I shall attempt to show, through a method called "Amerindian autohistory" (the study of correspondences between Amerindian and non-Amerindian sources), that the Native American cultural (or spiritual) being is as far from disappearing today as at the time of contact. Contrary to conventional historical discourse, my premise is that ever since the 'discovery' of America, world society has been engaged in a process of ideological unification that may be called simply "the Americization of the world," whereby the essence of original American thought is being communicated to the other continents. We are therefore facing a phenomenon of reverse assimilation, occurring at a rhythm dictated by history.

By studying what is original about Native American culture, and therefore about Native history, I shall try to show how modern American societies could benefit from demythologizing their socio-political discourse and becoming aware of their "Americity." That is, on this continent where they have just come ashore, they should see spirit, order, and thought, instead of a mass of lands and peoples to be removed, displaced, or rearranged.

METHODOLOGY

To impart the social nature of this view of history, I believe that it is extremely important to deal at the outset with the consequences of the upheaval produced in America by microbial infections from Europe. We must comprehend the extent of the epidemiological disaster before we can remove feelings of guilt and help to reconcile the two civilizations concerned, Amerindian and European; for, in accordance with Amerindian philosophy, people's feelings must be addressed before any question can be dealt with. In the second chapter, I shall discuss the Amerindian vision of life, the world, and creation, and through it the Amerindian matriarchal social system. The third chapter will study the essential Amerindian values, their persistence and universality, closing with a reflection on Amerindian autohistory and its social utility.

In the fourth chapter, I shall present what I see as the cornerstone of traditional northeastern Amerindian historiography, the destruction of Huronia by the Iroquois. My version will be based on primary sources such as the Jesuit *Relations* and, particularly, the writings of Father Joseph-François Lafitau. The fifth chapter will introduce the Baron de Lahontan, chronicler of the eighteenth century and founder of modern anthropology. I shall attempt to show how that controversial writer and his philosophical ally, Adario, were pioneers in the "Americization" of the world. The sixth and final chapter will show how, through autohistory, a contemporary nation – the Wendat (Huron) nation of Lorette – has discovered ways to defend itself.

In the conclusion, I shall discuss the responsibility of history to the future evolution of the human conscience, as well as the contributions Amerindian autohistory can make to this process.

The acted role of an Indian,
A character assumed wrong.
The continuous misinterpretations
Of a life
That is hurting.

Echoes climb,
Distorted
Endlessly by repeated lies.
An undertow of current time.

Will it ever die?
Loosen the bond.
Undo?
Will not this relating ease

So that we may rest,
Performance over
And unravel the mistake –
Stories told
Of Indians and white men.

Rita Joe, *The Poems of Rita Joe*
(Halifax: Abanaki Press 1978)

CHAPTER 1

DISEASE HAS OVERCOME THE DEVIL*

Over a 400-year period beginning in 1492, the aboriginal population of the American continent shrank from 112 million to approximately 5.6 million.[1] The population of Mexico, which numbered 29.1 million in 1519, stood at no more than 1 million in 1605.[2] As for North America alone, of its 18 million Amerindian inhabitants at the time of European contact, by 1900 only 250,000 to 300,000 descendants remained.

Contrary to widespread belief, the Amerindian wars, whose intensity was very slight before the Europeans arrived, were not the cause but the result of this depopulation – the most massive in known human history. By far the most important cause of the "American apocalypse" was the epidemic diseases brought by the

---

* This chapter should not be seen as an attempt to absolve the first European immigrants to American soil of the physical, moral, and spiritual atrocities committed against Native peoples, some of which are still taking place in the last "wild" confines of the continent. The key idea is that, had it not been for the European advantage created by the diseases that the newcomers imported in spite of themselves, the Native peoples would have had a chance to absorb the ideological and political shock, which would have been far less powerful. In addition, such an hypothesis questions the very motive for the arrival of Europeans in the New World; for, if Europeans had not for a very long time been largely isolated from the living forces of nature, they perhaps would not have been afflicted with the bacteria that eventually made them leave their own world.

newcomers.[3] The American demographer Woodrow Borah wrote in 1964: "The peoples of the New World and after them those of Oceania, who were living in complete or near-complete isolation, absorbed, in a few decades, the impact of all the diseases which could be disseminated. They received in a very short period, the series of shocks which Europe and the Far-East had been able to absorb over several millennia."[4]

In 1992 North America will have undergone five centuries of continual destruction of its human, animal, and plant populations and of its physical landscape. For five hundred years, both those who brought the bacteria and those who were almost completely wiped out by them have been on trial. To my knowledge, however, the bacteria themselves have never been tried, although the benefits of such a procedure, which are of two kinds, could be tremendous.

First, in terms of the ecological awareness the human race is now seeking to create, a study of why such a fertile bacterial culture was present in one of the two worlds, yet was at the same time non-existent in the other, could lead to a rediscovery of the laws that govern a healthy relationship between human societies and nature. It could also lead to an understanding of the causes (and consequences) of the rupture between societies and nature when people forget those same laws. It is a matter of learning a new attitude towards life and the universe by studying the spiritual essence of America.

Second, in terms of discovering a new social ethic, putting the microbes on trial instead of their carriers has the great advantage of removing the burden of guilt from humans who are merely the victims of these pathogens. Since first coming into contact, both carriers and receivers have suffered from an inability to recognize the true instigators of the great disaster in which they have been plunged; to recognize this situation would serve, not only to indict the guilty party, but also and most importantly to enable all of us to work together towards a reorientation of human thought. Until now, the discourse on the politics of ecology has been incomplete, since the citizen of Earth who probably has the best knowledge of solutions – the New World Native – has been systematically excluded from it. We must have faith in human solidarity against the microbes that have turned the inhabitants of the Old World into guilty parties and of the New World into victims. Now that humanity is logistically – and therefore socially – unified on a global scale, if we are to construct a responsible society, we must start by reflecting on what may have caused and still causes the social and ecological degeneration so typical of Old World and Euroamerican societies and so obviously absent from New World civilizations. Because we all have the power and the duty to help our fellow human beings to survive, a study of the original American philosophy could help to place attentive people at the heart of major forthcoming discoveries in the social sciences. Let us talk a little about the process of shedding guilt which this vision of history proposes to stimulate.

Amerindians always say that to attain reason, one must first treat the emotions with honour and respect. To gain someone's trust or cooperation, or to comfort others so as to have them participate in a shared objective, "it is necessary to deal in the first place with the emotions [of people], to lift up the spirits so as to sit down [together] and think clearly."[5] At the beginning of a speech or negotiations, northeastern Natives, particularly the Wendat-Iroquois, almost invariably offered several wampums, the effect of which was meant to "call reason back to its seat."[6]

For five centuries, Amerindians and Whites have dealt with their emotions only very sporadically and superficially. Society's interests, as defined by the dominant governments, have never allowed them to do more. Division was the rule, so that it was essential to produce and maintain emotional confusion by instilling feelings of guilt or superiority, prophesying, and so forth.

WHEN VICTIM BECOMES GUILTY PARTY

Many wars have been instigated both between Amerindians and between Amerindians and Euroamericans, and these conflicts have been largely used to conceal the demographic catastrophe created by the epidemics. Instead of trying to bring about a rapprochement between the cultures by describing the microbial impasse experienced by the Amerindians, attempts were made to justify the land-grab by telling how the bad Indians, especially the Iroquois, destroyed dozens of nations every years. In the *Relation* of 1649, Father Paul Ragueneau wrote:

By roads which covered a distance of about three hundred leagues we marched, upon our guard as in an enemy's country, – there not being any spot where the Iroquois is not to be feared, and where we did not see traces of his cruelty, or signs of his treachery. On one side we surveyed districts which, not ten years ago, I reckoned to contain eight or ten thousand men. For all that, there remains not one of them. Going on beyond, we coasted along shores but lately reddened with the blood of our Christians ... Alas, that those wretched Iroquois should have caused such desolation in all these regions ... Our sole consolation is that, having died Christians, they have entered on the heritage of the true children of God.[7]

Yet white men and red men alike were well aware of a far more pressing reason for the rapid annihilation of Indian America. The Jesuit Jérôme Lalemant wrote in 1640:

No doubt, they said, it must needs be that we have a secret understanding with the disease (for they believe that it is a demon) since we alone were all full of life and health, although we constantly breathed nothing but a totally infected air, – staying whole days close by the side of the most foul-smelling patients, for whom every one felt horror; no doubt we carried the trouble with us, since, wherever we set foot, either death or disease followed us ...

Wherein it must be acknowledged that these poor people are in some sense excusable. For it has happened very often, and has been remarked more than a hundred times, that where we were most welcome, where we baptized most people, there it was in fact where they died the most; and, on the contrary, in the cabins to which we were denied entrance, although they were sometimes sick to extremity, at the end of a few days one saw every person prosperously cured.

And the good priest added, praising the divine providence that manifested itself in those diseases: "We shall see in heaven the secret, but ever adorable, judgments of God therein."[8]

It is easy to see the missionaries too, Jesuits and others, as victims of the microbes they unconsciously helped to introduce, since their naive attitude was the product of a civilization that cared little for the laws of physical and mental equilibrium. It was not missionaries but diseases that overcame the Devil, of whom the Amerindians – worshippers of creation – were the brutish and happy slaves.

Red Rising Sun, a member of the Klamath nation, wrote in 1976 that "sin is correctly interpreted as the breaking of the laws of nature, and in consequence, man comes under the destructive natural forces, or Satan, and the form of suffering comes in a multiple array of diseases that can result in death. That the native nations of North America were innocently made to suffer the scourges of the white man's broken laws is cruelly evident as we look at recent North American history."[9]

CONCLUSION

Such a concept of history makes it possible to release the previously stifled emotions that keep people of all cultures from expressing compassion and respect, producing only guilt and hatred and preventing individuals from seeing their responsibility.

When wampums have been offered to all who are touched by history – to all human beings – whether to wipe away the tears that interfere with their vision, to ease their breathing, to render their ears sensitive again, or to smooth the paths of meetings until the beauty of life illuminates the eyes of all and reason, soothed, "comes back to its seat," then shall we be able to listen to and understand Amerindian autohistory.

CHAPTER 2

THE SACRED CIRCLE OF LIFE

According to the Sioux holy man Hehaka Sapa, everything done by an Indian is done in a circular fashion, because the power of the universe always acts according to circles and all things tend to be round:

> In the old days, when we were a strong and happy people, all our power came from the sacred circle of the nation and as long as the circle remained whole, the people flourished. The blossoming tree was the living centre of the circle and the circle of the four quarters nourished it. The east gave peace and light, the south gave warmth, from the west came rain, and the north, with its cold and powerful wind, gave strength and endurance. This knowledge came to us from the external world (the transcending world, the universe) and with it, our religion. Everything done by the power of the universe is made in the form of a circle. The sky is circular and I have heard that the Earth is round as a ball and the stars too are round. The wind whirls, at the height of its power. The birds build their nests in a circular way, for they have the same religion as us ... Our teepees (tents) were circular like the nests of the birds, and were always laid in a circle – the circle of the nation, a nest made of many nests, where the Great Spirit willed us to brood our children.[1]

The reality of the sacred circle of life, wherein all beings, material and immaterial, are equal and interdependent, permeates the entire Amerindian vision of life and the universe.

Every expression of life, material or immaterial, demands of the Amerindian respect and the spontaneous recognition of an order that, while incomprehensible to the human mind, is infinitely perfect. This order is called the Great Mystery. To the traditional Amerindian, life finds its meaning in the implicit and admiring recognition of the existence, role, and power of all the forms of life that compose the circle. Amerindians, by nature, strive to respect the sacred character of the relations that exist among all forms of life.

Where their human kin are concerned, the Amerindians' attitude is the same: all human beings are sacred because they are an expression of the will of the Great Mystery. Thus we all possess within ourselves a sacred vision, that is, a unique power that we must discover in the course of our lives in order to actualize the Great Spirit's vision, of which we are an expression. Each man and woman, therefore, finds his or her personal meaning through that unique relationship with the Great Power of the universe. There is no room for a system of organized thought to which the individual is subordinate, in the way that religions or political ideologies are at the service of human and material interests. "The duty of a man," states an Ojibwa medicine man with simplicity and all the depth of his respect for his tradition, "is to work for the Great Spirit."[2]

Human beings have an obligation to discover their own vision, their meaning, their religion; woman, with her special powers of self-purification, recognizes her vision much more easily than man does. With their awareness of the sacred relations that they, as humans, must help maintain between all beings, New World men and women dictate a philosophy for themselves in which the existence and survival of other beings, especially animals and plants, must not be endangered. They recognize and observe the laws and do not reduce the freedom of other creatures. In this way they ensure the protection of their most precious possession, their own freedom. Long ago, the independence of Amerindians was directly related to the incomparable abundance of food to which they had access. Henry F. Dobyns offers a startling and meticulous description of the food resources available to Natives of the Atlantic coast of Florida, sketching what he calls "the Native American Paradise Lost."[3]

The Amerindian originally lived in a world that recognized and honoured the spiritual uniqueness of each individual. It was of paramount importance for a male on the threshold of adulthood to penetrate the secret of his own spiritual essence – his vision – with the help of the appropriate exercises and rituals. The Ojibwa ethnologist Basil H. Johnston has written about the importance for the Native American to go on a vision quest and to obtain it:

Creation is, in the concrete, the fulfillment of the vision of Kitche Manitou (the Great Power) ... Every being, whether plant, animal or rock [is] composite (material and immaterial) in nature ... only men and women are endowed by Kitche Manitou with a capacity for vision; only man is enjoined to seek vision and to live it out ... Vision conferred a powerful sense of understanding of self and of destiny; it also produced a unique and singular sense of worth and personal freedom. Vision, when it did come, was the result of one's personal effort and maturation of the soul-spirit. As it was personal in terms of effort and as it represented a gift from the Creator, no one else was privy to it. There was to be in neither quest nor vision, interference ... The vision, when it did come, marked the culmination of the preparation and quest and the beginning of a new order of life ... No longer were the acts of a man or woman isolated deeds devoid of meaning or quality in the moral order. To life, there was purpose; to conduct, a significance in the fulfillment of the vision. No longer was true or applicable the dictum, "no man begins to be until he has received his vision." With the advent of vision, existence became living ... The Path of Life prescribed by vision was tortuous. Nevertheless, it was the mode by which men who received vision attained integrity, dignity, peace, fidelity and wisdom.[4]

The sacred circle of life, in which the place of humans is equal to that of the other creatures, albeit marked by a special responsibility, is divided into four quarters. Four is the sacred number in America: there are four sacred directions, four sacred colours, four races of humans, each with its own sacred vision, as well as four ages of human life (childhood, adulthood, old age, then childhood again), four seasons, and four times of day which are also sacred. Thus the circle operates in cycles of four movements each. When Amerindian officiants perform a sacred ritual whose primary function is purificatory, they mention and address themselves to those times or movements, and when they have covered the entire circle, they speak the words "all my relations," thus acknowledging the relationship between all beings in the universe and their common vision of peace.

THE ORIGINALITY OF AMERINDIAN HISTORY

In relation to the other continents, which are contiguous (with the exception of Australia), the American continent stands apart in the configuration of our world. The peoples of the Old World have always evolved in relative symbiosis, influencing one another in almost every way: economically, culturally, biologically, and so on. By contrast, until its definitive contact with Europe, the New World has been almost completely isolated, and so able to devise and preserve ways of being and living that are specifically its own. It has developed according to ideological concepts diametrically opposed to those that animated and motivated the Europeans and the other peoples who followed them here. In 1868 the ethnologist Daniel Garrison Brinton wrote: "Cut off time out of mind from the rest of the world, he [the American Native] never underwent those crossings of blood and culture which so modified and on the whole promoted the growth of the old world nationalities. In his own way he worked out his own destiny and what he won was his with a more than ordinary right of ownership."[5]

The same author also pointed out that, during the thousands of years when North America was free of outside influence, the continent became a surprisingly homogeneous linguistic "region":

> From the Frozen [Arctic] Ocean to the Land of Fire, without a single exception, the native dialects, though varying infinitely in words, are marked by a peculiarity in construction which is found nowhere else on the globe, and which is so foreign to the genius of our [English] tongue that it is no easy matter to explain it. It is called by philologists the polysynthetic construction ... It seeks to unite in the most intimate manner all relations and modifications with the leading idea, to merge one in the other by altering the forms of the words themselves and welding them together, to express the whole in one word, and to banish any conception except as it arises in relation to others.[6]

According to Université Laval linguist Pierre Martin, this striking particularity is still recognized by modern linguistics. It seems to indicate the existence of a conception of the world common to all Native American cultures; further, it helps to account for the fundamental unity of American philosophy, and to explain the absence from America of religious or economic wars. For the Amerindian, life is circular and the circle generates the energy of beings. Life is merely a great chain of relationships among beings. Humans acquire power only to the degree that they can channel and circulate energy (material and spiritual possessions). Pierre Clastres, in his book *La société contre l'Etat*, reports what Francis Huxley observed among the Amerindians of South America: "'It is the Chief's role to be generous and to give away all that is asked of him: in some Indian tribes, the Chief can always be recognized in that he owns less than the others and wears the most shabby ornaments. The remainder is gone in gifts.'" The situation,"Clastres continues,"is exactly the same among the Nambikwara described by Claude Lévi-Strauss ... There is no need to cite more examples, for this relationship between Indians and their chief is consistent right across the continent. Avarice and power are not compatible; to be Chief, one has to be generous."[7]

Amerindians have a fundamental respect for life and for the complementary nature of beings, who are all its forms of expression. They have no desire to affirm their supremacy over any other creature. They do not even domesticate animals, for animals, like humans, possess a spirit and liberty. The Amerindian does not exploit. Daniel Garrison Brinton further observed in America "the entire absence of the herdsman's life with its softening associations. Throughout the continent, there is not a single authentic instance of a pastoral tribe, not one of an animal raised for its milk, and very few for their flesh."[8]

ECOLOGICAL CONSTRAINTS PECULIAR TO AMERICA

Amerindians deserve no credit, of course, for the experience their continent has undergone. Civilizations are but the products of a chain of circumstances in the destiny of Earth, our common habitat; they are shaped by the constraints of climate and geography (for example, proximity to others, or states of isolation). Too often, when historians and social scientists try to explain the origins of human social evolution, they describe communal living as the primordial form of society. Nevertheless, superficial descriptions of this stage of evolution show that modern people have long since lost all notion of the intellectual and spiritual tools with which they could have preserved a dignified image of their past and thus of their own human nature. Moreover, they have been so blinded by a falsified, learned image of their material evolution that they have been unable to realize that the spiritual heritage they encountered on their "discovery" of America was one they too must have possessed at a certain period in the Old World – before they lost it because of the constraints that led to the development of their present type of civilization.

As for the Amerindians, when they found the Whites lost on the shores of their continent – the Great Island on the Turtle's back – they were in full possession of the spiritual gifts referred to earlier. Possessions and wealth circulated freely, according to the law of the great circle of relations. This was not so much because of greater morality among Amerindians than among Europeans, as because of the physical context – the geomorphological constraints peculiar to America.

Accordingly, all first-hand accounts state that the starving, frightened, intolerant people who began landing here in 1492 were received with respect and humanity. They found such harmony, liberty, and tolerance that many began to leave their homelands for the new world of America.

Although seriously threatened by the wars and diseases their pale visitors brought with them, the Indians, believing in the existence of a plan known only to the Master of Life, never rebelled against their fate. They defended themselves only when it was necessary, because Indians did not know "the art of war": they understood infinitely better the art of peace. Resolutely and generously, they undertook the task of "Americizing the White Man,"[9] that is, doing everything possible to help this new child discover the essential, primordial wisdom of the new Earth-Mother he had just found.

THE AMERINDIAN IDEA OF CREATION

All Amerindians worshipped the Great Spirit, the Great Mystery, the Great Power, the Sky, the Master of Life, whom they called either Father or Grandfather, not so as to masculinize the Creator, but to represent the ultimate creative and protective force, source of all life and all power.

More concretely, all Amerindians refer to the earth as their mother, composed like them of body, mind, and spirit. The spirit that governs the earth and materially produces life is feminine. To the Wendat, the earth was created by a woman named Aataentsic, who came from a celestial world. The Great Turtle took her onto his back and ordered the animals to spread there a small amount of earth brought up from the bottom of the sea. The woman, together with the two sons to whom she soon gave birth, founded and arranged Earth for the human race. The two sons vied with one another to impose their personal notion of what human life should be: one, who was too good, wanted it to be easy, while the other strewed it with obstacles and dangers. Their mother caused balance to prevail, and so the human world became what it is: a place of beauty and order, but one where the ordeals that are part of the human condition encourage compassion, a fundamental moral dimension of life.

To the Amerindian, woman represents reason, the being who educates man, orients his future, and anticipates society's needs. Man acknowledges in woman the primordial powers of life and a capacity to understand its laws. As regards the organization and direction of society, the role assigned to woman is in a sense superior to that of man. This is most evident in "matriarchal" Amerindian societies, but it is equally true for those called "patriarchal," including most nomadic societies. These must follow a patrilinear order when founding their institutions – because of man's preponderant role in the material and spiritual quest for the vital necessities – but they are not in fact patriarchal. There is only an outward appearance of masculine power; the sense of closeness to the earth is reinforced by an awareness of direct dependence on its vital products (which, like humans, are born of the earth). It may be advanced that the vast majority of the nomadic peoples of America are matricentric in their ideological and spiritual conception of the world.

Unlike Wendat-Iroquois culture, which possesses agriculture and the trading power that it brings, members of nomadic societies are obliged to remain in a purer and more intimate harmony with the spirit of the earth and its children – animal, plant, and others. Nomads are more closely tied to their mother, the earth, than are the semi-sedentary. Their culture is centred on lightness, in every sense of the term: that is, it requires an optimal harmony. Their highly complex ideology is more alert to the forces of the universe. They are wise and peaceful, like all those who are close to nature, but in a particularly exemplary way.

THE MATRIARCHY

Johann Jakob Bachofen has described the matriarchy, or "gynecocracy," as he termed it, as a stage in human evolution, with any deviation from it representing an imbalance: "We have stated [previously] that the gynecocracy was the poetry of history; we may add that it represents the period of profane intuition and of religious premonition. It is the time of piety, of superstition, of wise moderation, of equity. All these qualities, engendered by the same principle, are attributed by the Ancients, with surprising unanimity, to the gynecocratic peoples without distinction."[10]

Amerindian societies, so steeped in the great circle of relations, are only very rarely patricentric. To support the thesis of widespread matriarchy among prehistoric Amerindian populations, some authors have tried to establish a close relationship between the process of acculturation following epidemiological depopulation and the erosion of matrilinearity. As historian Shepard Krech III argues:

> Comparative data from outside the Northern Athapascan region suggest fairly precise connections between the intensity of acculturation pressures and the erosion of matrilineal descent principles within two generations, and the substitution of neolocal for matrilocal postmarital residence in the same time span ... The more acculturated members of a society may abandon matrilocal practises and matrilineal ideologies and terminology in favor of bilateral and generational systems prior to less acculturated members; or the more acculturated members may simply not be interested in traditional practises.[11]

In gynocentric societies, Bachofen writes, "all men are brothers, all women are sisters, until the victory of patriarchy undermines the homogeneity of the masses and replaces confused uniformity with consistent grouping. Whence freedom and equality, which are typical traits of so-called gynecocratic civilizations; similarly, kindness to strangers and aversion to restrictions of any kind."[12]

According to Amerindian gynocentrist thought, the patriarchal theory of evolution, no matter how refined and intellectualized, is nothing but an apology for racism, sexism, and what we term "androcentrism," defined as an erroneous conception of nature that places man at the centre of creation and denies non-human (and indeed, non-masculine) beings their particular spirituality and their equality in relation to life's balance.

Modern woman longs for the day when "woman's persevering influence, rejecting the false and the conventional which are in a sense man's trademark, will rediscover the true paths of nature."[13] This woman finds her most powerful inspiration in the Amerindian woman. It was a Jesuit, Father Lafitau, who first revealed to the world the essence of democratic American thought when he observed the matricentrist mechanism that is the real basis of Iroquois society, since it represents the key to the remarkable social equilibrium of Amerindian societies. Speaking of Iroquois women, he said in 1724:

> Nothing is more real however than the women's superiority. It is they who really maintain the tribe, the nobility of blood, the genealogical tree, the order of generations and conservation of the families. In them resides all the real authority: the lands, fields and all their harvests belong to them; they are the souls of the councils, the arbiters of peace and war; they hold the taxes and the public treasure; it is to them that the slaves are entrusted; they arrange the marriages; the children are under their authority; and the order of succession is founded on their blood. The men, on the contrary, are entirely isolated and limited to themselves. Their children are strangers to them.[14]

On the different conceptions of feminine law held by Europeans and Amerindians, this missionary to the Huron and Iroquois noted that in those nations the man must offer a considerable gift to the house of the woman he wants for his wife:

> The present made by the husband to his wife's lodge is a true coemption by which he buys, in some sort, this household's alliance. There is this

difference [from the Roman custom of coemption] that the husband gives the present whereas, with the Romans, the wife gave it, giving three marked cents, as the symbol of this coemption. The reason for this difference is that, with our Indians, the wives are mistresses and do not go away from their homes, while, with the Romans, they went into the house and under their husband's jurisdiction, so that they had to buy the right to be mothers of a family.[15]

This deference towards the woman reflects the recognition, in matricentric societies, of a human brotherhood vested in the Earth-Mother, source of respect for personal vision in those societies. Non-Native writers still frequently do not perceive this fundamental cultural difference. Instead, they tend to insist on depicting Amerindian societies, especially hunting societies, as being governed by the naturally more imposing men, whereas the reality is quite different. Bachofen, again, offers his thoughts on gynocentric societies, characterized by order and gentleness, as compared with androcentric societies characterized by harshness and moral confusion:

The cult of reproductive maternity gave way to that of sterile pleasure. For man, sex is for his pleasure, while for woman it is the duty of procreation sanctified by suffering. Under her reign, perpetuating the species had been the dominant preoccupation, imposed by an exclusively moral force with chastity as a necessary and inevitable condition. Man made selfish debauchery the supreme good, establishing his excess as natural law, using, to satisfy them, the brutal constraint imposed by his more vigourous muscles. This dual, contradictory tendency of the sexes is indisputable; it is still apparent today in everything they say and do; male domination has instilled in our civilization and our morality a profound corruption that erodes and dries up the sources of life, lowering happiness to the basest forms of pleasure. The masculine motto continues to be: War and Lust, the feminine: Continence and Peace.[16]

The "high status" of Amerindian women is not, as some authors have declared, "the result of their control over the tribe's economic organization."[17] The matricentric thought in these societies springs from the Amerindian's acute awareness of the genius proper to woman, which is to instil into man, whom she educates, the social and human virtues he must know to help maintain the relations that are the essence of existence and life. Women do not control anything through some "force" they possess, as Judith K. Brown would have it; they act through the natural intuition which Creation communicates to those who are open to its laws. Man, as Bachofen observes, does not possess this genius for educating: "It is by caring for her child that woman, more than man, learns how to exceed the narrow limits of selfishness, to extend her solicitude to other beings, to strive to preserve and embellish the existence of others."[18]

When he is in command – which itself is a departure from nature – man can only opt for material wealth, for he lacks woman's intimate understanding of the price and value of life. He bases his power on brute force. Woman, however, naturally opts for peace and stability; her power is founded on the education of the inner strength (the quest for vision). Woman's thoughts are long, out of concern for humanity; man's are short, a result of personal and national pride.

Natural man, that is one who belongs to a matricentrist society, entrusts his seed to woman, who conceives, nourishes, and educates it. Thus filled with goodness, humanity, and gratitude, man cheerfully carries out his role as protector. Throughout time, a large part of the spiritual burden of gynocentric societies is that Earth, a woman, is under the domination of patriarchal man.

Georgina Tobac, a sage of the Dene nation, crystallizes in one sentence the anguish experienced by the Native when the earth is assailed by modern man: "Every time the white people come to the North or come to our land and start tearing up the land, I feel as if they are cutting my own flesh; because that is the way we feel about our land. It is our flesh."[19]

CONCLUSION

When fifteenth- and sixteenth-century Europeans, products of societies in which oppression was the norm if not the rule, came to America, they found territories, villages, towns, and cities organized in such a way as to respect the circular chain of all orders of life, notably the four elements that correspond to the four cosmic directions. While these Native nations were not exempt from the dissent, conflicts of interest, or armed confrontations that are peculiar to human nature, none of them tried to impose the philosophical or religious principle whereby man *and not woman* can and must exploit the non-human beings that are necessary for their survival until they have been exhausted.

The multimillenial Amerindian experience demonstrated the great circle's civilizing potential, as well as the personal strength of the individual who finds his or her place within it.

CHAPTER 3

THE AMERINDIAN IDEA OF BEING HUMAN

THE ESSENTIAL AMERINDIAN VALUES

The portrait of a culture depicts the ideas that are most important to its people. The hierarchy of priorities is called a scale of values; culture, therefore, is fundamentally a question of values.

To understand the values that have motivated a people in its relations with another people or civilization, it is essential to comprehend the values of the cultural groups concerned. This makes it possible to respect the motives and recognize the dignity of those peoples. As Bruce G. Trigger states:

> The differences between large-scale and small-scale societies are sufficiently great that an historian's experience and personal judgement are not enough to permit him unaided to come to terms with the ideas and values that were a part of the Indians' way of life prior to the coming of the Europeans. Unless the historian is able to acquire elsewhere sufficient knowledge of the beliefs and values of the people he is studying, he is unable to evaluate the European sources which constitute the principal record that we have of these peoples. Lacking such knowledge, he is further unable to transcend the prejudices and limitations of his sources and to evaluate them in the rigorous manner with which historians wish to deal with all written material. It is precisely because most historians lack such knowledge that the Indian does not come alive in their writings,

no matter how sympathetic and well-intentioned they may be. The historian's dilemma is thus the lack of a technique which will permit an understanding of Indian ways without having records written by the Indians.[1]

This chapter aims at fostering an understanding of how Amerindian societies perceived the ways that have traditionally permitted their cultures to survive. It also refutes the old arguments about their inevitable disappearance, and shows that the Amerindian oral and written tradition may inspire the creation of new techniques of historical investigation and compensate for the absence of "written records." As Trigger suggests, the impressive baggage of myths and prejudices carried by average Euroamerican historians prevents them from turning to modern Amerindian society as a place where, far from their paper laboratory, they might imagine formulas that could make ethnohistory (an interdisciplinary method for studying the history of ethnic groups) into a major social science.

AMERINDIAN AUTOHISTORY

In 1974, historian Donald B. Smith wrote in his conclusion to *The "Savage"*: "If we aim at depicting the past of Native peoples in a realistic way, it is indispensable that we know in detail about their beliefs and customs. When they have left few or no written documents, it is necessary to resort to their oral tradition. Historians must associate themselves to both traditions and documents and know *the men as much as the archives*."[2]

Amerindian autohistory is an ethical approach to history, based on two premises. First, in spite of European appropriation of Native territory, Amerindian cultural values have influenced the formation of the Euroamerican's character more than the latter's values have modified the Amerindian's cultural code, since it was not the Amerindians who left their natural surroundings. Second, history is not yet aware that studying the persistence of essential Amerindian values, through testimony by the Amerindians themselves, is more important in relation to the *social* nature of historical science than are the frequent analyses of cultural transformations, which are technically interesting but too often of negligible social impact. Ben Kroup, a New York State anthropologist, very clearly describes the responsibility of the professional "who gets paid to interpret [Native] cultures": "Archaeologists, museum types, most historians seem to be object or document-oriented – they don't normally deal with flesh and blood people." Later, he adds that he has not "learned from the [Seneca] consultants, the things that usually interest anthropologists, such as cultural determinants, relations with other traditional systems, songs, dances, etc.," but that he did "learn, which is probably more important, the values, the ideals, the goals of the politically conscious Iroquois of today." History, he continues, "isn't worth doing if it isn't tied to current realities. In fact, it can't be done. You can't divorce the creation – the writing – of history from contemporary hopes, fears, problems. Mainstream America has so much to learn from the Six Nations ... If we ever face the reality of our 'contact' with the Iroquois over the last three and a half centuries, we may have a chance as a civilization."[3]

We note at the outset that, from the Native point of view, the persistence of essential values is more important than change, just as from the non-Native point of view, it has always been more interesting to shore up the myth of the disappearance of the Amerindian. If we accept the two premises of our historical approach, however, we can see how important it is, at both the historical and the social level, to know who the Amerindians are and what they can continue contributing to the non-Amerindians.

An examination of the Amerindian philosophical tradition will show the persistence, vivacity, and universality of the essential values proper to America. Using this tool for increasing non-Native awareness, we shall be able to show that if history is to be sensitive to society's needs, it must also study and reveal to the dominant society what is salutary, instead of continuing to talk about "primitive" cultures that are dead or dying. Such history is socially irresponsible, pointless, and misleading. History written in that way is like a shell without its animal content: its subject is matter, not thought.

In short, Amerindians think that while they have changed, like everything in the world, they are still themselves. Their vision is the same: they maintain their respect for the earth, which stirs them far more than, say, Star Wars, for which they do not have the slightest admiration.

Amerindians are naturally given to reflect on the order of life (the circle) and the purpose of things. They do not see history as a meaning that humans can confer on life; for them, the sense of life is, instead, the liberty of every being. They believe that humans do not make life, but that life makes humans. To Amerindians, the theory of evolution signifies the human being's authority over time; history as imposed on Amerindians represents the outsider's refusal to let them fulfill their vision. Trying to understand life's teachings means following its movements; caring only for recording the "facts" in order to remember them means choosing stagnation over movement, the profane over the sacred.

THE UNIVERSALITY OF AMERINDIAN VALUES

As Rémi Savard, the great Québécois scholar of the Amerindian, acknowledges in *Destins d'Amérique,* "The genuine American dimension, which is still appropriate today to the peoples born on this continent, is neither English, French, Indian, or Inuit; it is contained in the Native concept of the 'Great Circle,' following which an obsessive respect for the specificity of each link becomes the indispensable condition for the integrity of the whole. We no longer have a choice; it is that America where we must seriously consider disembarking, at last."[4]

What accounts for the remarkable strength of Amerindian philosophy is the capacity of *all* Amerindian nations to agree about the unity and dignity of *all* beings. When Amerindians gather their thoughts before praying, they address greetings to the whole universe. That reminds them of their place within creation; as an Onondaga spiritual chief explains, "We are not the rulers ... we must work together in order to continue ... We are sitting (when we assemble) with the Great universal Circle of Life. We are all equal, Life is all equal."[5]

The Amerindian respects life in all its forms. Among Prairie cultures, the officiant in the ritual sweat lodge pays homage to the fire-reddened stones at the moment they are taken from the lodge through a door reserved for them: "Thank you, sacred relatives, for having helped your human kin purify themselves through contact with the Eternal Forces. Continue, now, your existence, while we, your grateful relatives, live. Thank you, sacred relatives."[6] The Sioux sage Okute explained in 1911 that "when a medicine man says that he talks with the sacred stones, it is because of all the substances in the ground these are the ones which most often appear in dreams and are able to communicate with men."[7] Consider, as well, the following story:

> The elder Alexander Henry recalled the scene that followed his shooting of a hibernating female (bear). "The bear being dead, all my assistants approached, and all, but more particularly my old [adopted Ojibwa] mother ... took her head in their hands, stroking and kissing it several times; begging a thousand pardons for taking away her life; calling her their relation and grandmother, and requesting her not to lay the fault upon them, since it was truly an Englishman that had put her to death."[8]

Accounts such as these take on added meaning when it is remembered that the American Natives' reverent attitude towards animals could not be separated from their recognition of the precious nature of *human* life.

As for the spirit world, Ojibwa holy man Peter Ochees insists that souls be considered and seen as, quite simply, relatives. Amerindians spontaneously acknowledge the existence of a world governed by spirits, and communication with them is a normal exercise of their own spirits, for they are also related to that world. The American Indian, writes Calvin Martin, "lived more or less in what we would call a mythic world."[9] He continues: "It seems to me that the entire text of that history [of the Amerindian] – all 500 years of it – must be rendered so as to include this cosmological perspective ... if Indian behavior is to make any sense at all."[10] He concludes: "Perhaps in the process of finding him [the Amerindian as he defined himself and his world], we will discern another meaning for this land, as well. In a very real sense, the meaning of the New World still awaits our discovery."[11]

The Amerindians' declaration of their affection for the earth is universal. In all regions of the Americas, at all times, only the words change. The expression is all the more emotional as the danger of seeing their lands taken away or destroyed becomes more imminent. In the early 1900s, the Sioux chief and orator Luther Standing Bear echoed the feelings of all his Native brothers in the Americas:

The Lakota was a true naturist – a lover of nature. He loved the earth and all things of the earth, the attachment growing with age. The old people came literally to love the soil and they sat or reclined on the ground with a feeling of being close to a mothering power. It was good for the skin to touch the earth and the old people liked to remove their moccasins and walk with bare feet on the sacred earth ... The soil was soothing, strengthening, cleansing and healing.

That is why the old Indian still sits upon the earth instead of propping himself up and away from its life-giving forces ...

Kinship with all creatures of the earth, sky and water was a real and active principle ...

The old Lakota was wise. He knew that man's heart away from nature becomes hard; he knew that lack of respect for growing, living things soon led to lack of respect for humans too. So he kept the young people close to its softening influence.[12]

THE PERSISTENCE OF AMERINDIAN VALUES

To avoid idealizing Amerindian society, it is appropriate, before we describe in more detail the values stemming from the Amerindian notion of a universal relationship among all beings, to point out an essential difference between Native societies and the European ones that settled in the New World. In *Le pays renversé*, Denys Delâge draws an important distinction between the two types of civilization:

War (as noted by a Huron visitor to France) is no longer outside, it exists *between* Frenchmen: the enemy is within. While in Huron society all members of the tribe are part of the collective entity, such is not the case among the French, where torture, incarnating the king's omnipotence, serves to instil fear and resignation in the dominated classes. Beyond the apparent similarity between torture on the two sides of the Atlantic, the choice of victims as well as the whole symbolic structure of the ritual refers to altogether different functions.[13]

This idea matches the description given by Pierre Clastres of the nature of coercive power in "historic" societies:

Political power, like coercion or violence, is the mark of historical societies, that is of societies that bear within them the cause of innovation, change, historicity. Societies could thus be arranged along a new axis: those with non-coercive political power are ahistorical societies, those with coercive political power are historical. This arrangement is quite different from the one dictated by the present reflection on power, which identifies societies without power and societies without history. Innovation, then, is the foundation of coercion, not of politics.[14]

Coercion and war, as both these authors note, are virtually absent from natural societies. While Amerindians never inflict great harm on one another during "wars" between distinct nations or tribes, neither are they constantly or universally at peace with their human brothers. Conflicts exist, and enemies sometimes treat one another with extreme cruelty. Within a nation, however, feelings of love for one's fellow humans, and feelings of respect and solidarity, meet the commandments dictated by the law of the sacred circle of relations. All the virtues associated with the notion of kinship are illustrated in a noble and admirable fashion. Such admiration, moreover, runs through the accounts by all European observers during the early days of contact, from Christopher Columbus to Martin Frobisher. They lack words to describe the goodness, the generosity, what they perceive as the Christian charity of these peoples, which were astonishing to any European; of course, they also deplore, with compassion, the fact that God is not yet known to them.

In 1648, the Jesuit Paul Le Jeune expressed the admiration that many Europeans, in the early days of contact, felt for Native people:

It seems as if innocence, banished from the majority of the Empires and Kingdoms of the World, had withdrawn into these great forests where these people dwell. Their nature has something, I know not what, of the goodness of the Terrestrial Paradise before sin had entered it. Their practises manifest none of the luxury, the ambition, the avarice, or the pleasures that corrupt our cities. Since Baptism has made them disciples of the Holy Ghost, that Doctor is pleased to be with them; he teaches them, far from the noise of tribunals and of Louvres; he has made them more learned, without books, than any Aristotle ever was with his ponderous volumes.[15]

Within their own society, which in many cases is a confederation of societies, Amerindians genuinely embody all the personal and social virtues generally attributed to the "noble savage." Typically, they have great respect for the person and for all forms of life, and are temperate, modest, true to their word, honest, zealous on behalf of the common good, and courageous under trial to the point of heroism. They see to it that the dead are respected, the weak protected. They are generous to strangers, spontaneously seeking to integrate them within their extended families. They are polite, do not interrupt, never become angry, and have a high regard for individual freedom. In short, they are in every respect civilized beings, educated by nature itself; above all, they show utter ease and confidence in their society's values. All in all, the attributes of the "bad Indian" apply to Amerindians only when they engage in vindictive action against a social group that – temporarily, for peace is always feasible – is not part of their communication and trading networks. Marshall D. Sahlins's description of the African Bushman applies fully to the American Native. "The worst thing, says the Bushman, is not giving presents. If people do not like each other, but one gives a gift and the other must accept, this brings a peace between them. We give what we have. That is the way we live together."[16] Peter Wraxall, a writer in colonial New York, attributed to Amerindians the aphorism: "Trade and peace are to us one and the same thing."[17]

Amerindian society is extremely close-knit; each individual receives the attention and affection he or she requires. Everyone has an equal place in the social circle and everyone protects with equal devotion the security and quality of social life they take from it. Consequently, treason, aside from witchcraft, is generally the only offence liable to punishment by death. "In this country," wrote the Jesuit Pierre-François-Xavier Charlevoix during the 1740s, "all men believe themselves equally men and what they most value in man is the man. There is no distinction of birth, no prerogatives attributed to rank which cause prejudice to the rights of individuals; no preeminence attached to merit, which inspires arrogance and makes others too conscious of their inferiority."[18]

Very early in the history of the contact between Amerindian and European civilizations, European authorities grew alarmed at the attraction that the Amerindian's free and unconstrained way of life exerted upon Whites, though they could do nothing about it. In 1685, to his great regret, the governor of New France had to write to the Marquis de Seignelay, his superior in France: "It was believed for a very long time that domiciling the savages near our habitations was a very great means of teaching these people to live like us and to be instructed in our religion. I notice, Monseigneur, that the very opposite has taken place because instead of familiarizing them with our laws, I assure you that they communicate very much to us all they have that is the very worst, and take on likewise all that is bad and vicious in us."[19]

Towards the end of the seventeenth century, a Micmac chief gave the Recollet priest Chrestien LeClerq his opinion of the French in the following terms: "There is not one Indian who does not consider himself infinitely more happy and more powerful than the French."[20] The accounts by Europeans at all periods since their discovery of the New World are filled with testimonies by Amerindians expressing faith in their cultural vision, which focuses on the development of the human being, as well as their almost total lack of confidence in European ethics.

The Inuit people exemplify a nation who, to survive in the far north, have given the fullest meaning to the sacred circle of life. Characteristically, the Inuit give the most complete expression to their practise of the social virtues. Their great cordiality towards strangers and their cultural mechanisms for integrating them into Inuit society reflect unlimited confidence in their own values. This anecdote by an unknown Inuit writer from northern Quebec illustrates that people's attitude: one that is proud and not easily impressed by material considerations external to their philosophical notions:

It is written in books that we Eskimos was [*sic*] always confident in ourselves. Even during the time of exploration of white men in our country our Native people really showed their capabilities. One time an aeroplane landed in a small village in Northern Canada. It was the first time our people ever saw one. The crew or pilot of the plane bought whole lot of fur from our people, and one of our people wanted to buy the plane, (since he had a lot to sell) the pilot said to him even if you bought it you would not be able to fly it because you never saw one before; and the Inuk said: 'If you can fly it, I can.' Such is the attitude that we must always have. Want to be a Premier? You can be! Want to be an Astronaut? You can be![21]

A similar confidence in his people's values and traditions was expressed by the Seneca chief Red Jacket:

When asked ... in 1824 why he was so opposed to missionaries [Red Jacket] replied ... The Red men knew nothing of trouble until it came from the white men; as soon as they crossed the great waters they wanted our country, and in return have always been ready to teach us to quarrel about their religion. Red Jacket can never be the friend of such men. If they [the Indians] were raised among white people, and learned to work and read as they do, it would only make their situation worse ... We are few and weak, but may for a long time be happy if we hold fast to our country, and the religion of our fathers.[22]

In contrast to the case of Europeans and the inhabitants of other continents who have left and continue to leave their countries of origin in large numbers, to come and live on the red man's soil, history reports no cases of Amerindians voluntarily leaving their continent on a permanent basis. The Amerindians' attachment to their land, and their unique relationship with it, is the source of their remarkable faith in their values. The great majority of Amerindian nations firmly believe that progress as understood by the dominant civilizations, wherein humans are lords of creation devoid of conscience, will one day end, and then the Amerindian will be responsible for recommunicating to the other peoples of the earth a social system based upon an understanding of the circle. Abraham Burnstick, a Cree-Assiniboine holy man from Alberta, talks about a pre-Columbian prophecy transmitted to him by his grandfather:

Another people shall come, from beyond the salt water, which will take the lands away from the Amerindian peoples and, by means of a drink, try to erase their minds. The Old ones used to say that that drink was snake blood. They knew that the Amerindians would accept this drink from that stranger and that they would thus die in great numbers, to the point of almost becoming extinct, but that in a future time, soon after a time when machines would start carrying men in the sky, the Native people would give back to the stranger the ill-fated drink and would begin to walk straight once more, to think correctly and to play a dignified and most beneficial role in the world. We have arrived at that time.[23]

In 1970, Hopi spiritual chiefs revealed their own conception of their global role to a mining development company that was in the process of destroying a large part of Hopi and Navajo lands:

We, the true and traditional religious leaders, recognized as such by the Hopi People, maintain full authority over all land and life contained within the Western Hemisphere. We are granted our stewardship by virtue of our instruction as to the meaning of Nature, Peace, and Harmony as spoken to our People by Him, known to us as Massau'u ... Today the sacred lands where the Hopi live are being desecrated by men who seek coal and water from our soil that they may create more power for the white man's cities. This must not be allowed to continue ... The Great Spirit said not to take from the Earth – not to destroy living things. The Great Spirit, Massau'u, said that man was to live in Harmony and maintain a good clean land for all children to come.[24]

At a 1977 United Nations conference in Geneva, where traditionalist Amerindian delegates presented the cohesive and salutary contents of their philosophy and prophecies, the Sioux holy man Wallace Black Elk summed up the feelings of his fellow Amerindians as follows: "Even if there is only a slight chance of encouraging human beings to live according to the Red Way, which is the right way, we shall seize that opportunity and we shall educate our own people, and the Americans and all the peoples of the world. That is why we come to Europe, to educate and re-educate the people so that they will go back to the original instructions."[25]

At the same conference, spiritual leaders of the Hodenosaunee (the Iroquois Longhouse) spoke in the name of the natural world as follows:

> The human species today is facing the very question of its survival. The way of life known as western civilization is setting out along a road of death where its own culture has no viable responses. Faced with the reality of their own destructive capacity, they can only advance towards ever more effective zones of destruction ...
> The great majority of the world has its roots in the natural world, and it is the natural world, with its traditions, which must prevail if we want to develop societies that are truly free and just ...
> The peoples who live on this planet must do away with the narrow concept of human liberation and start to see that liberation must be extended to the whole of the natural world. What is needed is the liberation of all things that maintain life – air, water, trees – all the things that maintain the sacred web of life ...
> We believe that the Aboriginal peoples of the western hemisphere can go on contributing to the survival potential of the human species ...
> The traditionalist Aboriginal peoples hold the key to reversing the gears of western civilization which promises a future of untold suffering and destruction. Spirituality is the highest form of political consciousness. And we, Aboriginal peoples of the western hemisphere, are among the surviving Keepers of this type of consciousness. We are here to communicate that message.[26]

THE VIGOUR OF THE AMERINDIAN CONSCIENCE

Many fundamental psychological traits have inevitably been suppressed in the ordinary behaviour of Amerindians. These traits still underlie their mentality, however, and have a powerful effect on the expression of their character, besides determining its nature. There are two reasons for this. The first is, quite simply, the attachment of Amerindians to ancestral values. The second, more significant, is the Amerindian awareness that the cultural habits associated with those values have been suppressed in a completely illogical and unjust manner. I believe that this explains both the Amerindians' singular awareness of their duty to remain, essentially, Amerindian, and the persistence of a particular ideological portrait. In the words of Onondaga Chief Oren Lyons, being Indian in America has, fundamentally, nothing to do with the supposed material or physical characteristics of the "Indians" of old.

> We have lost our old ways, but the principles that we go by are not old: peace is not old, justice is not old, equity is not old, it's what everybody aspires to. Those [things] are ours ... Old is in the mind of the person, old is in their education. We're contemporary people. I don't apologize for standing in these clothes today, for that's what I wear. This is me, this is the Hodenosaunee right now, right here ... we don't expect to see [former U.S. president Ronald] Reagan with a white wig.[27]

Historian John Mohawk also talks about the non-Natives' crystallized perception of Amerindians: "[The greatest specialists of our history] have said that we are only the *descendants* of the Iroquois ... that we have ceased to exist theoretically in 1784, or 1789 ... that we are now inadequate, somehow ... that Indian culture now lies under a glass dome."[28] He adds: "Ours is a brilliant culture. Our people has so much to inform the world about; about how a people can move in the world successfully."[29]

Jean Raphaël, sage of the Montagnais nation and former chief of the Mashteuiatsh nation in Lac Saint-Jean, comments in general terms on the responsible attitude of northern Amerindian hunters towards the environment and animals: "They [Amerindians] took very good care of nature ... We have never destroyed in the way you see non-Indians doing today ... I wish I could teach all those people how to protect and preserve nature, how to cultivate the hunting lands." Then, describing the basic nature of the Amerindian, Raphaël recounts certain episodes from his own life that shed light on the foundations of Canada. Speaking of parishes which he saw being established, he says that it was a natural impulse for the Amerindians to go and help the "poor settlers." "The Indian has always been generous," he adds, revealing his personal feelings about his people.

As for the persistence of Amerindian culture, Raphaël declares that "the Indian will always continue to identify himself as an Indian. Amerindian languages are becoming vigorous again. In a word, as long as the Indian is in Canada he will remain Indian: that won't change ... The Indian is a founder of Canada ... The character of the Indian is rather unusual: he is always prepared to give. He is always keen to meet [a fellow man, no matter who he is] and help him."[30]

On the vitality of Native society, during a dance in which several villages from his native Vancouver Island participated, the writer, actor, and painter George Clutesi observed:

In my time, we nearly vanished from our own land ... Many of us [our villages] throughout the entire west coast of Vancouver Island grew very weak in my time, and it was partly because we forgot our own songs, and didn't dance our own dances for the longest time. Until 1949, it was totally against the law for any of you, for any of us, to sing our own songs, or dance our own dances and we are grateful that these laws have been repealed ... We are beginning to know each other much more than we did then.[31]

Through their music and poetry and their arts in general, the eastern and northern nations also express a keen awareness of their Amerindianness. The Montagnais poet and thinker Armand Collard gives metaphorical expression to the contemporary thought of the Amerindian people about their history:

From time out of mind you, old brother [Amerindian] and your sister, Nature, have lived on this part of the continent that is called North America.

Do you recall a very distant time, at the dawn of the world? You and your sister were free to live a healthy life that you prized greatly ...

But one day something happened, other persons came to join your deeply united family ...

They arrive, take, destroy. It is all done so quickly you have no time to react and so you submit. It is very easy to understand that, for you, it may seem inconceivable.

Today, those strangers would have you believe it is you who are the stranger.

Never forget that this Earth you tread has been trodden by your forefathers ...

They come to you with a shiny, artificial future [financial compensation] which they offer in exchange for your mother, the Earth.

Walk with your head high, for you are sovereign, my Idlu [Montagnais] brother.[32]

In 1967, the Micmac poet and songwriter Willie Lawrence Dunn presented his Native version of the Canadian national anthem:

O! Canada!, our Home and Native Land,
One hundred thousand years, we've walked upon your sands,
With saddened hearts, we've seen you robbed and stripped
Of every thing you prized

While they cut down the trees,
We were shunted aside to the jails and penitentiaries.
O! Canada!, once glorious and free,
O! Canada!, we sympathize with thee,
O! Canada!, we stand on guard for thee.[33]

Another poet, Eléonore Sioui Andatha of the Wendat nation, presents the universal message of her people very clearly in *The Huron are Rich (Oukihouen Wendat)*:

In the Amerindian
Are found
The tears, smiles, cries
Of the soul of Mother-Earth
For he was born of her –
Made fruitful by the sun –
Amid a rustling of the Spirit
Encircling his brothers
In his new birth.[34]

Revitalization of Native American thinking is a continent-wide phenomenon, particularly in Central and South America where the population of many countries is principally Native. It is growing in proportion to the development of ecological awareness on a world scale.

In Argentina, the Native musical group Taki Ongoy restates a Peruvian theory from the 1560s which claims the moral superiority of traditional Native thought and announces its awakening after a period of lethargy under the grip of the Spanish religion. In a song entitled "Taki Ongoy," the group affirms:

They have taken from us the earth and the sun,
Our wealth and our identity,

Now all that remains is to forbid us our tears,
To wrench from us our very hearts.
Cry with me, cry Taki Ongoy,
That through your voice our race will live again,
Cry with me, cry Taki Ongoy,
For our America is Indian and of the sun.[35]

In a recent article in its official periodical, the World Council of Indigenous Peoples presents the following Amerindian reaction to Spain's planned celebrations of the five hundredth anniversary of the arrival in North America of Christopher Columbus:

The Spanish media inform us of the sumptuous preparations that country's government is making as 1992 approaches.
We don't want to spoil their party. What we demand is respect for our dead, at least through acts in keeping with historical truth. We demand that their development "aid" does not add to the misery that has been our lot for 500 years.
We form a society that has a history and that recognizes the inevitable evolution of things and of peoples. The Conquest is a reality which has already caused enough tears and blood to flow. The European presence on the so-called American continent is an irreversible historical fact; it serves no purpose to deny what already exists.
However, a celebration that is clothed in ruined party finery, which builds festive settings in graveyards, and which claims to blind and gag the truth with dollars is an offence upon which no future can be built. We cannot go back to live at Tenochtitlan or Saksayhuaman, but we can still erect a monument to justice, we can still build our future upon the recognition of truth. That would be a more enduring celebration.[36]

In the Amazonian jungles of Brazil, where some Amerindian tribes wear no clothes and still hunt with bows and arrows, there is also a revitalization of Native consciousness. A Brazilian anthropologist, recipient in 1978 of the International Award for the Promotion of Human Understanding, pointed out in 1979 that "the most important phenomenon to appear in the past five years is the ability of certain tribal groups to defend their interests with respect to the state and to organize themselves into larger units that go beyond tribal limits, with a view to creating an identity engendered by a kind of pan-Indianism, itself based on indigenous leadership, either pre-existing or newly created."[37]

This movement continues with vigour. Quite recently, in February 1989, the Kayapos of the Brazilian Amazon, in an attempt to block construction of an enormous dam, organized ("on their own initiative") an historic meeting that brought together five hundred representatives of thirty-eight Native nations and a hundred teams of reporters from forty countries. The Amerindians demonstrated a high level of ecological and political awareness, as well as exceptional independence towards the media. "For a long time," they declared in a letter read at the meeting, "the white man has attacked our thinking and the spirit of our elders. Now he must stop. Our territories are our people's sacred place, the inviolable dwelling of our Creator."

According to the Brazilian periodical *Afinal*, this unprecedented meeting of Native nations was "far more than a protest against construction of the Belo Monte dam on the Xingu river. It supported a concerned and categorical refusal of a hydro-electric complex that would be responsible for building seven power stations in the region by the year 2010, with direct, negative effects on seven Native societies already disgusted by the tragedies of Cucurui, Balbina and Itaipu."[38]

CONCLUSION

The technique of Amerindian autohistory is based on the premise that the study of Amerindian philosophy has a distinctive, dynamic dimension which represents, as Bruce G. Trigger suggests, "a potential source of insights into the human condition that comprehend those of the original culture and which may in due course have adaptive value for the whole society."[39] This technique assumes that historical science cannot ignore under any circumstances – at the risk of reproducing in other forms the prejudices that have characterized all its attempts to deal with societies without a written tradition – the ideas and feelings of the people who make up those societies today. This assertion is important, since it implies that non-Native researchers, because of their background, are less able than Amerindian researchers or traditionalists to comprehend the cultural modes specific to Amerindian societies. In fact, that is the feeling of most Amerindians towards any person from the outside who has not been "naturalized" in their fashion.

Our own autohistorical approach, however, recognizes that the didactic substance which must be delivered is addressed to the dominant non-Amerindian society. As soon as Native and non-Native specialists agree on that principle, they will also recognize that non-Native specialists naturally possess a superior ability for understanding how, to what extent, and at what rhythm their own society must be exposed to this didactic content. It is possible, therefore, to define a fair and ethical division of the responsibilities and prerogatives incumbent upon each member of this intercultural team. The technique of autohistory is also an attempt to create strategies for intercultural action that would give our society the power to use the enormous wealth represented by a knowledge of Amerindian history and philosophy.

If no fair or satisfactory historical evaluation seems to have come from the outside (heterohistory), the only remaining source is autovision or autohistory; this is a technique that aims, through a varied set of sources and categories of informers, to establish the constant cultural traits of one or more culturally related peoples. Such a method would be a basis for establishing a new history to match the image of themselves that people have always had, or should have.

The goal of Amerindian autohistory is to assist history in its duty to repair the damage it has traditionally caused to the integrity of Amerindian cultures. As for methodology, Amerindian history should be based on a delimitation and recognition of its ideological territory and its particular philosophy, taking into account the following factors:

- the absence – the eradication – of the vast majority of spatial and temporal data that might have provided an awareness and understanding of Amerindian social and cultural mechanisms;
- the natural inability of colonial histories to comprehend other cultural and social modes, and thus to incorporate in their dis-

course a valid ethical dimension, to ensure harmonization of the perceptions and relationships between the societies with which they deal;
- the need for the presence and commitment of the people whose traditions are being studied in the interpretation of their history;
- cultural and geographic specificity in relation to the other continents.

Once values that are strictly Amerindian – American – have been presented and recognized, they will serve as guidelines for defining the *new* historical field of Amerindian history. To start with a recognition of the Amerindian way of being, all the written data that have been used by the dominant society so far to write "the history of the Amerindian" should be revised and reinterpreted. No use can be made of these sources so long as the question "Who is the Amerindian?" remains unanswered.

In the history we are making, Native people, instead of being stepping-stones for "true civilization" in America, become the guides who will take their white visitors towards Amerindian civilization, a truer and more human one. Slowly but uninterruptedly, this culture has transformed and continues to transform the views and attitudes of all other civilizations, because it has refined the concept of the interdependence and brotherhood of *all* beings (not only human beings) to the highest degree.

In this chapter, we have sketched an "ideological portrait" of Amerindians. While it is neither elaborate nor definitive, we believe it is faithful to what they were at the time of European contact and to what they are today. We shall now turn our autohistorical method to a subject that has been a cornerstone for writing the kind of history taught in Euroamerican schools and colleges until now, namely the rivalry between Wendat and Iroquois in the sixteenth and seventeenth centuries.[40]

CHAPTER 4

THE DESTRUCTION OF HURONIA

In recent decades, a certain number of researchers have been critically examining George T. Hunt's theory that the Iroquois waged war for economic reasons. For Bruce G. Trigger, there is both a cultural and an economic dimension to the matter: he maintains that because the Five Nations did not possess the entrepreneurial tradition of the Wendat, they tried to increase their trading power by acquiring new hunting territories rather than trade routes.

Most recent studies, however, are closer to the older, so-called "cultural" theory advanced in the writings of Francis Parkman, which attributed the wars waged by the Iroquois on so many other Amerindians to an enmity that, under certain favourable conditions (for example, the European invasion), would lead to the annihilation of one party.

In addition, revision of the earliest Amerindian demographic data has led other investigators to explain the nature of these conflicts differently. One of these, Wichita University historian Karl H. Schlesier, in a discussion of the "legend" of Amerindian middlemen, says that "the Iroquois never attempted to become middlemen in the fur trade: neither did other Indian tribes, including the Huron or Ottawa. They all were touched by far more powerful forces than European trade goods."[1] He explains that "smallpox (the main epidemic disease brought from the Old

World) emerges as the most significant among those forces. Much of the historical and ethnological literature before and after Hunt propounds biases which not only do injustice to the Iroquois, but prevent a deeper understanding of the historical truth."[2] Most authors still present what we call "the myth of economic war," attributing to Native peoples on the brink of disaster the motives, interests, and intentions of people leading a normal existence. In fact, all Amerindians were waging desperate cultural war on an invader whose pathogenic allies made his very presence a disaster.

INTERPRETING THE FACTS ACCORDING TO AUTOHISTORY

Louis Hall Karaniaktajeh, a Mohawk artist and philosopher from Kahnawake, sums up the Amerindian's feelings about history with bittersweet humour: "Twistory," he says, "is written in such a way that you think that they [the colonizers] are heroes. They're out there plundering Indian land and looting, but it's their right, their God-given right ... and the Indians are not supposed to do anything about it, they're supposed to like it; they're supposed to even help the writers of these history books to plunder them."[3]

Of all Amerindians, the Iroquois are those who have least wanted "to help" the Europeans to "plunder" them, and for that very reason they spread terror and animosity among the first generations of Europeans to establish themselves in northeastern North America.

"The good Hurons were destroyed by the wicked Iroquois," we were led to believe from the time we were old enough to absorb prejudices, in order to distract an entire society from the real story of the grabbing of Amerindian land.

Always bearing in mind that microbes, not men, determined this continent's history, we shall use data provided by our Amerindian autohistorical analysis to try to elucidate the circumstances that enabled Europeans to destroy the order Amerindians had established for countless generations.

In 1492, the Wendat were situated geo-politically at the centre of a very important society of Amerindian nations. Wendake (the

Wendat country) was the heartland that was the origin and focus of the main trade networks linking this vast extended family of societies, whose spirit perfectly reflected the Amerindian's social ideal: interdependence and redistribution around the common circle.

We may assume that communications networks in the original Amerindian world, free of national boundaries, while they were far less rapid than today's, were functional and reliable, and that news about the Spanish military and epidemiological devastations reached the northern peoples after a few years at most.

In 1498, the Italian John Cabot reported having visited Nova Scotia and Labrador, while in 1501 the Portuguese Gaspar Corte-Real captured 57 Amerindians, probably Beothuks. When Jacques Cartier arrived in 1534, the Amerindians had already suffered from epidemic diseases brought by Europeans.

Some recent opinions, even when well-supported, do not sufficiently recognize the terrifying consequences for Amerindians of the Europeans' arrival. In "European Contact and Indian Depopulation in the Northeast: The Timing of the First Epidemics," Dean Snow and Kim M. Lanphear attempt to invalidate the hypothesis put forward by Henry F. Dobyns in *Their Numbers Become Thinned*, where he postulates on pandemics in the northeast during the sixteenth century. Moreover, they also appear to dismiss three fundamental considerations:

- First, while inland peoples such as the Mohawk – living in what is now the state of New York – could defend themselves against epidemics, coastal nations such as the St Lawrence Wendat-Iroquois, the Micmac, and the Montagnais, who inevitably came into contact with European crews, could not. In fact, while no ship went up the St Lawrence to Stadacona (now Quebec) before Jacques Cartier, a good number certainly did so during the rest of the sixteenth century.
- Secondly, the epidemic that ravaged Stadacona during the winter of 1535–36 (and that may well have had more than the fifty victims Cartier reports) was undoubtedly not the only one that occurred over the 115 years between the arrival of the first ships in the Gulf of St Lawrence around 1500 and the first "official" epidemic of 1616.

- Thirdly, both the very nature of the culture and way of life of these Amerindian societies, that is, their close union and the uniformity of their cosmo-political conception, encouraged the spread of contagious diseases.

Once these elements are considered, it is likely that the St Lawrence Wendat-Iroquois disappeared in the sixteenth century because of the epidemics that raged in the St Lawrence valley before the beginning of the seventeenth century.

In other words, depopulation of the northern part of North America had already begun in the sixteenth century, probably spreading panic through Amerindian society at large. Taioagny and Domagaya, the two sons of Donnacona, the "seigneur of Canada," made a forced journey to France in 1534, returning in 1535. Cartier thought that he could use them to disorganize the Amerindian country, but as it turned out they bore him a barely concealed suspicion. Better than anyone, these chief's sons were aware of the danger. Cartier left after having defied the Amerindian order, spurned their advice (which cost the lives of twenty-five members of his crew who, unprepared for the Canadian climate, died of scurvy at the beginning of winter), and captured the father of the two young men along with nine other members of their family, including at least one young girl.

While it is certain that the bulk of pre-contact Amerindian society did not live in perfect, constant harmony, archaeology informs us that those Amerindians did not experience significant conflicts, likely because they had the ideological and social means to maintain relative peace among themselves. "In every case," writes archaeologist James A. Tuck, "village and tribal movements A.D. 1000–1500 are devoid of drastic population shifts, conquests and the annihilation of whole prehistoric populations."[4]

It is very likely that the Wendat-Iroquois migrated north from southern countries, taking root fairly recently at the heart of the Algonquian world. Their way of life – they were farmers and traders with a remarkable gift for political organization – had enabled them, long before the Europeans arrived, to establish particularly harmonious relations with other nations. History and even pre-history prove beyond a doubt that the vast majority of the Algonquian nations had long since assigned the Wendat confederation a key role in the political, commercial, cultural, and religious sectors of a vast and strategically located territory.

It appears that at the time of European contact, the confederacy of the Five Nations Iroquois was the only one not yet integrated into this extensive trading system. Ironically, the people who originally were probably the least numerous and geo-politically the most marginal were the only ones able to resist the invader and provide a refuge for the survivors of previously stronger nations. In that way, the ideology common to all aboriginal nations was able to survive.

There is every reason to believe that the decimated residents of Stadacona, led to Wendake by Donnacona's descendants, as revealed by archaeology[5] – tried once they were resettled there to persuade the Wendats to form a great league of nations. It is conceivable that the central idea was open resistance to the pale and dangerous visitors and that, frustrated at having been ignored, a certain "prophet" named Deganawidah, a member of that ideological clan, had taken his message to the Iroquois nations. The latter, located outside the great Wendat trading network and thus spared the task of facing the Europeans head-on, were more receptive to the message.

According to Iroquois tradition, it was a Wendat – one "whose people had not wanted to listen to him" – who disclosed the prophetic message about the need to form the Iroquois league.

Most of the speculations by Elizabeth Tooker[6] as to when the Iroquois confederacy was founded place it around 1540–90, a period that corresponds fairly closely to the Wendat-Iroquoian exodus to Huronia.

In any case, the Wendat were traditionally considered as standard-bearers for the Amerindian ideology which claims that, if the world is to be and to remain what it is, it must be founded on communication and exchange between humans of all origins. The vision of a prophet of the resistance, no matter how enlightened, can never take ascendancy over the ideology of a society of nations that groups together hundreds of thousands of individuals, one that has always been nurtured at the inspiring, appeasing sources of the great circle.

In 1894, the historian J.N.B. Hewitt pointed out that "no league or confederation of peoples was perhaps ever formed without a sufficient motive in the nature of outside pressure."[7] We may assume that the Wendat, because of the refugees they took in by virtue of a clear cultural kinship (for example, the Stadaconans), or adopted, apparently by force (as seems to have been the case for at least part of the Hochelagans[8]), felt the need to reform their confederacy before the Five Nations Iroquois did, and this led to the consolidation of the Iroquois confederacy. As the Wendat were chiefs of the great Amerindian society of the northeast, they inevitably devised a union that was centred on trade. Naturally there was a place in it for the French and other Europeans, despite the disastrous consequences of their coming: it lasted about half a century, if we bear in mind that a pandemic in 1520–24 had "almost certainly reached the Seneca"[9] and other neighbours of the Wendat long before its European carriers arrived, and that yet another, between 1564 and 1570, had made them abandon some of their villages.

The Iroquois, realizing the extent of the disaster, opted for defence. By allying themselves against the French-Amerindian force, they now declared their dissidence from prehistoric political and trading organization. The Iroquois made the difficult but inevitable decision to embark upon a war they knew would be very long and destructive, and whose logic was utterly foreign to Amerindian thinking.

According to Amerindian cultural logic, the Iroquois were the northeastern nations best situated to resist the invasion, although they had virtually no chance of succeeding. Consequently, the Iroquois nations were no longer "the worst of all savages" or "the Indians of Indians" as they have so often been called. Instead, they were an extremely valorous people who, to enable the Amerindian race to survive, had to fight against the European powers, forcibly adopting nations that were already gravely decimated. For the Iroquois, the goal of this war was to extinguish the power of strangers in the way one extinguishes a raging fire. With extraordinary strength of character, they had to eliminate part of their own race so as to save it.

To explain the Iroquois' political offensive in relation to the French, historian John A. Dickinson quotes ethnohistorian Bruce G. Trigger: "The majority of Huron were killed or captured as a result of the general warfare that was going on between the Mohawk and the French; however, the emphasis that the Mohawk placed on capturing Huron prisoners reflected their long-term ambition to incorporate all of the Huron who had come to Quebec into their own society or, failing this, to kill them." "Thus," Dickinson observes, "the French would be deprived of allies."[10] He concludes by stating that when the Iroquois attacked Long Sault, they did not intend to destroy the colony by massacring the settlers, but to paralyze it by abducting most of the remaining Huron warriors – mercenaries in the service of New France. "If the [Iroquois] army went up the Ottawa River," Dickinson explains,

> it is because their goal was to take Annaotaha [the chief of the Hurons] and his companions; Dollard's band was completely outside the Iroquois' preoccupations. For seven years, the Iroquois had been trying by every means possible to destroy [that is, to take away from the French] the whole Huron colony and here, at long last, was the chance to do it. Marie de l'Incarnation was amazed that the enemy's army was content with "so few people," but the reason is that this small group was the quarry the Iroquois had been looking for. For the Iroquois, the meaning of Long Sault was not the defeat of the seventeen Frenchmen, but the annihilation of the remaining Huron warriors. For them, it was a great victory.[11]

In the final analysis, both the Wendat and the Iroquois realized that they could not unite, because of the age-old order of the country. The Wendat noted impassively that the end was rapidly approaching. They would never accept the numerous peace overtures by their Iroquois cousins, nor would they make the choice – which seemed to the Jesuits so logical – of eliminating those priests who "established themselves in the heart of the Country [Wendake] to better bring about its ruin."[12] The Wendat, like any people, were ineluctably caught in the logic of their civilization. They had to trade until the end, like beavers who will get caught in traps until they are extinct: they were victims of their own nature.

The historiographic concept of "the destruction of Huronia by the Iroquois" is an axiom in the traditional history of the northeast that justifies North American sociopolitical attitudes. In the light of Amerindian autohistory, this cliché becomes an example of the manipulation of history, absolving Europe (particularly France) of the destruction of the most politically significant aboriginal people north of Mexico, a people who best represented the Amerindian interethnic fabric in northeastern North America. This is a spectacular historic fraud: responsibility for the sociodemographic calamity in the northeast is assigned not to microbes, but to the Iroquois.

Karl H. Schlesier refers us to the Jesuits' pitiful descriptions of the Wendat and other nations in 1640, after several successive epidemics:

> Disease, war and famine are the three scourges with which God has been pleased to smite our Neophytes since they have commenced to adore him, and to submit to his Laws ... All these events have so greatly thinned the number of our Savages that, where eight years ago one could see eighty or a hundred cabins, barely five or six now can be seen; a Captain, who then had eight hundred warriors under his command, now has not more than thirty or forty; instead of fleets of three or four hundred canoes, we see now but twenty or thirty. And the Pitiful part of it is, that these remnants of Nations consist almost entirely of Women.[13]

Later, Schlesier asks, "Where after these tremendous losses, are the men supposed to have come from to fight continuous wars during this period? ... These wars sprung only from the imagination of scholars."[14]

TRADITIONAL AMERINDIAN VALUES OF THE WENDAT-IROQUOIS IN LAFITAU'S TIME

Our twofold aim here is an historical rehabilitation of the Iroquois, and a demonstration of their profound adherence to the Amerindian value system. Even if the defensive action of the Five Nations towards the Europeans – particularly the French – was basically a fight to the finish between two civilizations, the Iroquois continued to live according to essential Amerindian values. From what we know of the present vitality of Amerindian social consciousness, we can study a particularly revealing description of Iroquois (and, in secondary fashion, Wendat) cultural consciousness at the beginning of the eighteenth century, left by the Jesuit Joseph-François Lafitau.

This missionary, who lived among the Wendat and then among the Iroquois, knew these peoples intimately. His *Customs of the American Indians* is an unusually valuable account of their philosophy and spirituality.

Lafitau, whose church was facing a rise in religious skepticism, drew from the Amerindian peoples a series of arguments to support a thesis of many contemporary theologians concerning the innate existence of a religious sense in man. For thinkers of the time, the "sauvages amériquains" were "the humans who show themselves in the most simple form in which they can be conceived to exist."

To an informed modern reader, Lafitau's work may seem to go beyond his original objective. In reality, he contributed to alleviating the Amerindians' crushing historical burden and was one of the rare individuals who conceded them any right to survival. Moreover, Lafitau's work provides a solid mass of arguments and evidence that help restore dignity to the people descended from the "savage" nations Lafitau describes. Even more, he enables modern men and women to acquire or rediscover respect and a salutary admiration for human nature.

"Deganawidah [founder of the league of the Iroquois] brought a message of peace, say the contemporary Iroquois ... He devised the means of lifting up men's minds with the condolence ritual [addressing the emotions in order to attain reason], which provided for paying presents to the aggrieved. The same ceremony on a broader scale took former enemies into a network of alliances."[15]

The contemporary Seneca historian John Mohawk helps us penetrate deeper inside Iroquois thinking about their confederacy. He stresses the importance in Iroquois society of the development of oratorical art, since for them as for all Amerindians, no one has arbitrary power over any other person. Hence the importance of the art of persuasion. For John Mohawk, the "greatness" of the confederacy of the Five Nations comes from its high development of this art. He adds:

This greatness [of the oratorical art] is the very idea of the Hodenosaunee:

all human beings possess the power of rational thought; all human beings can think; all human beings have the same kinds of needs; all human beings want what is good for society; all human beings want Peace ... Out of that idea will come the power ... that will make the people of the Five Nations among the most influential thinkers in the history of human thought ... The basic fundamental truth contained in that idea is that so long as we believe that everybody in the world has the power to think rationally, we can negotiate with them to a position of Peace.[16]

Almost three centuries ago, Lafitau, like all contemporary observers of Amerindian society, emphasized how the Wendat and the Iroquois kept order in their councils. He was impressed by their confidence (which they still possess today) in the human's capacity for rational thought, provided that society respected individuality. "In general, we may say that they are more patient than we in examining all the consequences and results of a matter. They listen to one another more quietly, show more deference and courtesy towards people who express opinions opposed to theirs, not knowing what it is to cut a speaker off short, still less to dispute heatedly: they have more coolness, less passion, at least to all appearances, and bear themselves with more zeal for the public welfare."[17]

Faced with the Amerindians' choice of gentle persuasion in their relations with their fellows, as opposed to the coercive modes of European societies, Lafitau experienced the same sense of wonder as European chroniclers of all times:

While the petty chiefs of the monarchical states have themselves borne on their subjects' shoulders and have many duties paid them, they have neither distinctive mark, nor crown nor sceptre nor consular axes to differentiate them from the common people. Their power does not appear to have any trace of absolutism. It seems that they have no means of coercion to command obedience in case of resistance. They are obeyed, however, and command with authority; their commands, given as requests, and the obedience paid them, appear entirely free ... Good order is kept by this means; and in the execution of things, there is found a mutual adaptation of chiefs and members of society and a hierarchy such as could be desired in the best regulated state.[18]

By observing some of the social traits noted by Lafitau, we can better understand how the integrity of the human person, as well as the quality of relations between humans, are at the heart of Amerindian social ideology. He frequently contrasts Amerindian solidarity with the European competitive spirit:

They should ... be done this justice, that among themselves, they spare each other more than Europeans do. They regard, with reason, as something barbarous and ferocious, the brutality of duels and the ease of mutual destruction introduced by a point of honour badly misunderstood ... They are no less astonished by the indifference of the Europeans for their fellow countrymen, by the slight attention paid by them to the death of their compatriots killed by their enemies.[19]

Lafitau openly admires the strength of the Amerindian social fabric, source of the individual's keen respect for the private life of others. This helps explain the gift-giving mechanisms for preventing and settling conflicts.

THE AMERINDIAN CONFLICT

In Lafitau's day, Amerindian societies, especially the Iroquois and Wendat, were in profound political disarray because of the European presence. In this stormy climate, the missionary was much better able to portray the Amerindian character than if the time had been peaceful. Much has been said about Amerindian cruelty and torture. As the Iroquois of that period were the prototype of the "cruel American savage," they contributed, in spite of themselves, to the elaboration of that image, one that was later applied to all Amerindians. Using Lafitau's descriptions and observations, we will now present a brief analysis of this historiographical "knot."

In the Amerindian ideological universe, "war for the sake of war," to use Lafitau's expression, does not exist. War – if the term can even be used with reference to Amerindian societies – is always the result of disruption of the political order, provoked by an enemy agent. The Iroquois, like all Amerindians, resigned themselves to war while being fully aware of its gravity: "The Council," Lafitau reports, "decides on war only after considering the plan for a long time and weighing with mature consideration all the factors pro and con."[20]

Because Amerindians saw their compatriots as the ultimate wealth, war assumed a meaning for them that compels admiration. In the conflict between Amerindians and Euroamericans, the Iroquois, as the most engaged Native people, were the ones who most often went to war, and consequently they lost the largest number of members. It was logical, then, for these nations to try to capture replacements for those who had been killed or seized; thus they did not simply indulge in murderous expeditions, as we are often led to believe. "The loss of *a single person*," Lafitau writes, "is a great one, but one which must necessarily be repaired by replacing the person missing with one or many others, according to the importance of him who is to be replaced."[21]

On this matter, Lafitau shows us how, in a natural and matriarchal society, the women recognized as sages (matriarchs) have supreme control over even the nation's military affairs. When there is a loss of one or many persons,

> it is not up to the members of the same household [the longhouse, which among the Wendat and Iroquois could contain as many as two hundred people] to repair this loss, but to all those men who have marriage links with that house, or their *Athonni*, as they say; and in that fact, resides the advantage of having many men born in it. For these men, although isolated at home and limited to themselves, marry into different lodges. The children born of these different marriages become obligated to their fathers' lodge, to which they are strangers, and contract the obligation of replacing them; in this way the "matron" (matriarch) who has the principal authority in this household, can force these children to go to war if it seems best to her, or keep them at home if they have undertaken a war displeasing to her.
>
> When, then, this "matron" judges it time to raise up the tree again, or to lay again on the mat someone of her family whom death has taken away from her, she addresses herself to some one of those who have their *Athonni* at her home and who she believes is most capable of executing her commission. She speaks to him by a wampum belt, explaining her intention of engaging him to form a war party. This is soon done.[22]

When it is time to set out and capture replacements, the leader of the expedition (still according to Lafitau) makes a public prayer, accompanied by all his relatives, who have dressed and adorned themselves in their best attire, as is done at the farewell feast for one who is about to die – for going to war is going towards death. All those who remain in the village hasten to obtain a relic from those who are leaving, and to give them some present. "Together," Lafitau tells us, "they exchange robes, coverings, or whatever other goods they may have. A typical warrior, before leaving the village, is despoiled more than twenty or thirty times."[23]

For Amerindians, no success or victory is great enough to make them forget, even for a moment, the value of one lost human life. In their society, the cult of the human, or of being (as opposed to the cult of having), assumes its full force and meaning. Lafitau is astonished at their respect for the dead:

> They have such respect for each other that, however complete may be their victory, and whatever advantage they may have gained from it, the first sentiment which they show is that of grief for those of their people whom they have lost. All the village has to participate in it. The good news of the success is told only after the dead have been given the first regrets which are their due ... The women do the same thing in regard to the men who have gone hunting or to war. For, at the moment of their return, they go to wait for them on the shore. And in place of showing (them) the joy which they must feel at seeing them arrive in good health, they begin by weeping for those of their relatives who died in the village during their absence.[24]

THE TREATMENT OF CAPTIVES

Of all the Amerindians, the Iroquois are known for the intensity of their defence against the crushing European invasion. For two centuries, from 1500 to 1700, they had to concentrate their strength in order to maintain the existence of a union of Amerindian nations. In response to the formidable onslaught of the epidemics, to say nothing of the European ideological assault, they developed a policy of adoption: as stated earlier, their "wars" against the Wendat and their allies aimed above all at restoring their own numbers.

In Native societies in general, war, "established by the need to protect oneself from injustice, to repulse force by force and to right the injuries which the tribes might have received from each other, [is] also sanctified by religion."[25] Yet for the Amerindians, war, as made known to them by the White man, never became the exercise of destruction and extermination it represents for other cultures. In 1609, Champlain was indignant at the behaviour of the Wendat and Montagnais, who cried victory when the Mohawk fled after a French musket-shot cost them three of their chiefs. Champlain did not comprehend why his Amerindian allies did not set out in pursuit of the Iroquois, to exterminate them to the last man; he claimed that the Wendat and Montagnais were "cowards" who "know nothing about making war."

But it is the Amerindians, not the Europeans, who have been given the title of champions of cruelty in the history books. This view is wrong. Amerindians never inflicted torture on anyone because of religious or political ideas. During the two hundred years of the crusades, millions of people were killed because they did not share the crusaders' beliefs. To establish a point of comparison with America, the Dominican bishop Bartolomé de Las Casas wrote in 1552: "We furnish as a very sure and true number, that during the said forty years (1492–1532), have died because of the said tyranny and infernal works of the Christians, unjustly and in a tyrannical manner, more than 12 million persons, men, women, and children, and I believe, trusting that I do not err that it was, in reality, more than 15 million."[26]

As for the Amerindians, if one of their warriors took a human life he did so only to gain respect for his nation, following a process always marked by the same humanity that characterizes his social vision of the great circle. Lafitau, in fact, recognized the rationality of the Amerindians' behaviour: "If they did not return the same treatment to those who treat them inhumanly, they would become their dupes, and their moderation would only serve to harden their enemies. The gentlest people are forced to put aside their natural gentleness when they see that it becomes a pretext for barbarous neighbours to become prouder and more intractable."[27]

The Iroquois themselves – and Lafitau supports them – deny being crueler than any other nation, White or Amerindian. Latifau wrote: "The Iroquois, so fearsome to the French on account of the great number[28] of those they caused to perish in these frightful tortures, have gained an even worse reputation with us than all the other tribes ... To hear the Iroquois speak, however, they claim to be less cruel than the others and treat the captives thus only by reprisal."[29]

Their treatment of captives shows the very humane nature of the Iroquois people, even in the midst of the catastrophe represented by European interference in Amerindian society.

Returning from a capture expedition, those who had captives to offer clans who needed them gave them away ceremonially. "The warriors who give a slave [more correctly, a captive]," Lafitau recounts, "award him with their belt which has served as a symbol of his engagement in their enterprise, or serves them as parole, to say that they have fulfilled their obligation."[30]

Among the Iroquois in particular, it was very unusual for prisoners – who had been captured with such difficulty, and whose lives were eminently precious to a nation so frequently decimated – to be condemned to torture by fire. Indeed, their fate would have stirred the envy of more than one hostage of a "civilized" country. Lafitau tells us that, after being handed over, "the captives are led to the lodges to which they have been given and introduced ... There, they are immediately given something to eat. The people of this household, however, their relatives and friends, are still weeping for the dead whom these captives replace, as if they were losing them entirely, and in this ceremony shed genuine tears to honour the memory of those persons, to whom the sight of these captives recalls a bitter recollection, renewing their grief in their loss."[31]

The adoption was then formally carried out, in a way that shows that the Amerindian social ideal is based and focused on maintaining and developing relations between humans, as well as on faith in the capacity for reasoning of all humans, so long as their dignity is recognized. Lafitau observes:

Among the Iroquois and Huron, it [the condition of "slave"] is gentler in proportion as that of those thrown into the fire is more cruel. The moment that he enters the lodge to which he is given and where he is to be kept, his bonds are untied ... He is washed with warm water to erase the colours with which his face was painted and he is dressed properly. Then he receives visits from relatives and friends of the family into which he is entering. A short time afterwards a feast is made for all the village to give him the name of the person whom he is resurrecting. The friends and allies of the dead man also give a feast to do him honour: and from that moment, he enters upon all his rights. If the captive is a girl, given to a household where there is nobody of her sex in a position to sustain the lineage, it is good fortune for this household and for her. All the hope of the family is placed in this captive who becomes the mistress of this family and the branches dependent on it. If the captive is a man who requickens an Ancient, a man of consequence, he becomes important himself and has authority in the village if he can sustain by his own personal merit the name which he takes.[32]

CRUELTY

The severity of Amerindian punishment should not be seen as cruelty, madness, or blindness. On the contrary, it was compassionate, logical, and rational, and was dictated by the Amerindian's unshakeable morality, modelled on nature herself.

If we avoid sentimentality, cruelty can be evoked only in the context of aggression and domination, and not self-defence. It is therefore absurd – and unfair – to talk about the cruelty of persons who are only defending themselves, for such cruelty is a legitimate and noble act of physical self-protection, as well as an equally noble effort to safeguard the honour which has been imperilled by the assailant's deed. Cruelty is therefore an argument to justify aggression, which is itself linked to a desire for domination or, in other words, destruction, partial or total.

Among Amerindians, human sacrifice did not have the character of social diversion it had for the Romans. Even less did it represent a punitive act that was religious or political in nature. Torture was, indeed, intended to be a way of killing the war itself; to achieve this, harshness was the best guarantee of success. By aiming violently at the actual enemy, it imposed respect and restraint, and so can be considered a more humane response to violence than are the conventional means used by so-called civilized societies.

In 1626, in view of the difficulties presented by the conversion of Natives, Father Joseph Le Caron warned the young priests whose ambition was to die as martyrs in Canada: "The general opinion [of Amerindians] is that one must not contradict any one, but leave each one have his own thinking. There is, here, no hope of suffering martyrdom: the Savages do not put Christians to death for matters of religion; they leave every one to his belief."[33]

The cruelty of the Amerindian was simply political. Once again, Lafitau helps us penetrate to the core of Amerindian philosophy through a description of the scene preceding the torture of an enemy by the Iroquois. "From the appearance of everyone assembled around a wretch who is going to end his days in the most horrible torment, we should guess that there is no question of such a bloody tragedy as is about to take place before their eyes. All exhibit the greatest calm in the world. They are seated or lying on mats as they are in the councils. Each one talks loudly with his neighbour, lights his pipe and smokes with the most marvellous tranquillity."[34]

Among Amerindians, the sacrifice for political reasons of a human being was devoid of hatred or sadism. It was a considered, rational, and necessary act. The person to be tortured was fully aware of this and did not try to elude his fate. "In the intervals in which they are left in repose," reports Lafitau, "they talk coldly of different matters, of news, of what is happening in their country, or they inform themselves calmly of the customs of those who are busy burning them."[35]

The Amerindians' well-known heroic steadfastness under torture results from an unshakeable faith in their moral and spiritual values. Lafitau, like all missionaries, admires them for that: "This heroism is real and the result of great and noble courage. What we have admired in the martyrs of the primitive church which was, in them, the result of grace and a miracle, is natural to these people and the result of the strength of their spirit. The Savages, as I have already shown, seem to prepare for this event from the tenderest age."[36]

Just as victims showed great dignity and courage, so did those who had to sacrifice them show their compassion, proving once more the centrality of the human being in the Amerindian social vision: "When a captive is burned among the Iroquois," Lafitau notes, "there are few who do not pity him and say that he is worthy of compassion. Many ... have not the courage to be present at his execution ... Some ... give him relief when he asks for something."[37]

CANNIBALISM

The French philosopher Michel de Montaigne claimed that "there is nothing barbarous or savage in that nation [Amerindians], from what I have been told, except that each man calls barbarism, whatever is not his own practice; for indeed it seems we have no other test of truth and reason than the example and pattern of opinions and customs of the country we live in."[38]

The notion of cannibalism as practised by "primitive" cultures is a product of the racist thinking of so-called civilized societies. In a society where the human being was at the centre, how did one dispose of the body of the individual who had to be tortured? How was the dignity of the human race to be preserved?

We know that evoking the Amerindians' bloody cruelty was a powerful means used by the colonial (mainly religious) authorities to attract the favour, sympathy, and financial support of their country's upper classes. Aside from this self-seeking attitude, some sources, particularly oral accounts, indicate that torture and its corollary, cannibalism, never had the importance attributed to them. Besides, our autohistorical study of Amerindian philosophy has provided ample evidence to destroy this fable.

One fact is certain, however, and it deserves the greatest respect: Amerindians did sometimes consume one or several parts (for example, the heart) of the body of a prisoner who died a particularly courageous death. The Amerindian gesture of consuming human flesh was as consistent with their conception of the great circle as was their proverbial generosity. When they had to defend themselves against their fellow humans, they did not like to kill instantaneously or massively as is done with mechanical weapons. They preferred to glorify their captive enemies in death by giving them the chance to die courageously. The remains of a life thus ennobled until death and in death could not be simply thrown away as garbage; they deserved to be eaten. Amerindians had to treat with honour the flesh of those whose lives they had

had to take. They consumed it because they thought they must: they had been required to destroy persons who, deep down, they admired and loved because they were brothers, whose hearts were filled with love, trust, and veneration for their Creator, and thus for their fellow human beings.

MORALITY

In his *Customs of the American Indians*, Lafitau compares Amerindian morality favourably with European. He maintains that Amerindian moral force invariably diminished upon contact with Whites. He talks about the northern nomads as being "more distant peoples, who are fortunate enough not to know us [Europeans]."[39]

Amerindians practised to a high degree those individual and social virtues known as Christian. According to Lafitau, they were charitable: "If a household of famished people meets another whose provisions are not entirely exhausted yet, the latter share with the newly-arrived the little food which they have left, without waiting to be asked, although in so doing, they are left exposed to the same danger of perishing as those whom they are helping at their expense, with such humanity and nobility of soul. In Europe under similar circumstances, we would find little disposition to such noble and magnanimous generosity."[40]

Similarly, their courtesy to visitors should be edifying to people of any culture: "Whoever enters their homes is well received," Lafitau observes. "The one who arrives or comes to visit has scarcely entered than food is put before him, without saying anything: and he himself eats without ceremony, before opening his mouth to declare the subject which brings him."[41]

RESPECT BETWEEN THE SEXES

The Amerindians' modesty and their discretion in matters of sex are well documented. Lafitau recounts customs that fell into disuse because of the example of the French. One such custom, according to Latifau, was "to pass the first year after the marriage without consummating it. Any advance made before that time would be insulting to the wife and would make her think that the alliance was sought less because of esteem for her than out of brutality."[42]

Another Amerindian custom, still practised among the Iroquois and others, does not allow an individual to marry another member of the same clan. This is true even if the person has been adopted by the clan, "for," as Lafitau explains, "since by giving them life the name of a particular person of this family is revived in them, they are given all the rights of adoption and represent those being resurrected as if they were those people themselves."[43]

The Amerindian of Lafitau's time would break off his intimate life with his wife as soon as a pregnancy occurred; "the general rule for all Savages is to stop living with their wives from the moment they declare themselves pregnant."[44]

BEING FAITHFUL TO ONE'S WORD

Lafitau cites an "old Huron" who told him that "it was a law from time immemorial in their country that a village had a right to put to death anyone who ... did not fulfil the obligations of his pledge."[45] Friendship is sacred among Amerindians. The ties that bind friends together are stronger than the ties of blood. An individual cannot marry a friend's relative, since the bonds of their friendship make them kin. Usually, Lafitau tells us, "friends follow each other to the stake."[46]

RESPECT FOR ANCESTORS' SOULS

Finally, Amerindians were admired by the first Euroamericans, especially the priests, because of their remarkable devotion to the souls of their dead. To the missionaries and perhaps more particularly to Lafitau because of the thesis he was defending, this natural disposition of the Amerindian was proof of the immortality of the soul, and so of the existence of God. Echoing numerous European observers, Lafitau wrote:

> It could be said that all their work, all their sweating and all their trade comes back almost solely to doing honour to the dead. They have nothing precious enough for this. And so they sacrifice their beaver robes, maize,

axes, and wampum, in such quantity that it could be believed they attach no importance to them, although they constitute all the wealth of the country. They can be seen almost naked in the winter cold, while they have, in their chests, good fur or woolen robes destined for the funeral duties. On these occasions, each person makes it a point of honour or religion to appear liberal to the point of magnificence or prodigality.[47]

CONCLUSION

Despite historians' tendency to produce an image of the Amerindian that serves the interests of colonialist societies, Amerindian ideology has lost nothing of its essence. To cite historian Robert E. Berkhofer, "The remarkable persistence of cultural and personality traits and ethnic identity in Indian societies in the face of white conquest and efforts at elimination or assimilation"[48] is proof that America has never had and will never have any lasting spiritual culture other than its Native one. White America has lost the cultural battle it waged against the Amerindian people. Most ironically, the Iroquois nation, which has most often served as a pretext for Whites to denigrate the aboriginal population, is now recognized even internationally as one of the most vibrant Amerindian cultures in the Americas. According to Mohawk historian and journalist Doug George, the Iroquois possess "an innate gift for organization." "You can find innumerable references in the historical documents that demonstrate the ability of the Iroquois people to pull it out of the fire, when things look their darkest, to create something out of that."[49] He points out that the Iroquois periodical *Akwesasne Notes*, founded in 1968, is "a device created [by the Iroquois] that has given stimulus to Indian movements across the hemisphere."[50]

Historically, the Iroquois' vision of peace was not limited to the Native people of North America, but has always been universal. To cite George again: "In 1656, a Mohawk delegation ... went to Quebec City and asked the French [who had the technology to do it] to take this message of Peace throughout the world ... to bring all the Nations together at Onondaga, under the Great Tree of Peace ... These were people who were gifted with world vision 300 years before the Europeans finally, after two world wars, stumbled across it."[51]

Today, the Iroquois still acknowledge "the duty of trying to reach the non-Native world as well." George adds that "even on the other side of the [Atlantic] Ocean ... we can see the influence of the Confederacy in movements like the Green Party that's taking hold among the young people of Europe, transcending national boundaries, an expression of the concern [in] those nations that they have 'a responsibility for their generations up until the seventh generation' [following the Amerindian maxim]."[52]

This triumph of Iroquois traditionalism, despite the fact that Amerindian culture has been severely undermined by the shock of contact, is proof enough in our opinion of the solid strength of America's original philosophy.

CHAPTER 5

LAHONTAN: DISCOVERER OF AMERICITY

Using cultural data provided by the autohistorical method, this chapter offers a brief examination of the thought of the Baron de Lahontan.

Louis-Armand de Lom d'Arce was born 9 June 1666 in the French province of Béarn, heir to the barony of Lahontan. Reversals of fortune, quite frequent among the upper classes in the so-called civilized states, led the young baron to leave his ruined family at the age of seventeen and come to help the colony of New France in its attempt to suppress the Iroquois enemy, the chief obstacle to the achievement of French hegemony in North America.

Young Lahontan's bitterness and his independent nature, along with an intelligence that was a felicitous combination of strength and refinement, made him remarkably able to capture and decode the essence of the American way of being, and to offer the greatest minds of Europe, then intellectually and theologically darkened, an enlightenment they could recognize. In fact, Lahontan's work had an indisputable and undisputed influence on the greatest thinkers of his day: Rousseau, Voltaire, Chateaubriand, Diderot all drew on him abundantly. Leibnitz, the great German philosopher, maintained a correspondence with Lahontan that indicates not only his keen interest in the latter's ideas but also a genuine friendship and respect. When in Europe, the baron enjoyed the favour, respect, and protection of the Dutch salons and of the English, Danish, Swedish, and German courts.

Publication of Lahontan's work brought a chorus of protests from supporters of the old political and religious doctrine, with people in both France and New France going so far as to deny its validity. In 1983, the historian Jacques Collin wrote: "We have observed the eclipse of Lahontan in Quebec. Think of his influence on the thinkers of the Enlightenment and we realize that history has not done him justice."[1] Traditional historians have been quick to denounce Lahontan's errors (sometimes, it is true, his statements may seem like pure inventions) and his most insignificant weaknesses. We will, for our part, counter conventional historiography in trying to establish, through our autohistorical approach, the fundamental authenticity of Lahontan's famous *Dialogues avec un Sauvage*.

I shall attempt to rehabilitate Lahontan's historical and social work at another level. My observation is based on the agreement between Amerindian thought, as revealed by the autohistorical method, and the voice of Lahontan, which frequently echoes the Amerindian's and justifies the baron's title as "the discoverer of Americity." Almost three hundred years ago, Lahontan wrote books that were revolutionary not only because of their ideas but even more because of the unique power they drew from the culture of a "new" continent. His was a courageous undertaking, and it brought him resentment and persecution by one of the most powerful social and religious establishments of his day. Condemned a thousand times, Lahontan is still waiting to obtain justice through testimonies by his chosen brothers, the Amerindians.

LAHONTAN AND ARISTOTLE

The philosopher Montaigne was both an assiduous reader of the Jesuit *Relations* from America, which shed light on the ideological and cultural distinctiveness of the peoples of that continent, and an ardent defender of the cultural and philosophical dignity of aboriginal American societies. More than a hundred years before Lahontan, Montaigne already sensed that American thinking could triumph over the well-established traditional ideologies.

"This is a Nation, I should say to Plato," wrote Montaigne, "in which there is no sort of traffic, no knowledge of letters, no science of numbers, no name for a magistrate or for political superiority, no custom of servitude, no riches or poverty, no contracts, no successions, no partitions, no occupations but leisure ones, no care of any but common kinship, no clothes, no agriculture, no metal, no use of wine or wheat."[2]

In 1711 Leibniz, sensing the political implications of Lahontan's ideas, wrote to his compatriot, the philosopher Friedrich Bierling:

> It is true that there are [American] peoples who live in societies without government and who are not tormented by the spur of cupidity. While they are, however – and this is certain – astonishingly susceptible to insults, ambition is unknown to them. It is necessary, too, that the moderation of their character be great, for they do not give themselves up to rage under the impulse of amorous rivalry that brings the very beasts into conflict, nor do they quarrel after drinking. Long ago Tacitus, speaking about the Germans, made reference to their frequent brawls while in a state of intoxication; there is nothing of the sort among those whom we most unjustly call Savages. We must admit that these people possess things we would be entitled to disbelieve had we not learned of them in certain fashion. Nor should we hold it against Aristotle and all the other political authors that nowhere did they foresee the existence of such a social system. However, we consider that their error must serve as a lesson to us, so as not to take strong likelihoods for demonstrations.[3]

THE FATE OF LAHONTAN'S WORK

Of all the literary works that reached Europe over the three centuries of European "conquests" of America, that of Lahontan unquestionably enjoyed the greatest success. According to Réal Ouellet, a Lahontan specialist at Université Laval, twelve years saw the production of "eight new editions or forgeries, translations into English, Flemish and German, as well as several reviews and discussions – often controversial and from very different perspectives." Yet, he notes, his work is "barely mentioned in intellectual or literary histories,"[4] a punishment his French compatriots inflicted on Lahontan for his sin of "sincerity." He was seen as a traitor to his country and his church. It was said that "he tears France apart; he looses his fury against the Powers most worthy of respect."[5]

In fact, Lahontan did not loose his fury against anyone: he had simply discovered another truth. Indeed he was like so many Europeans (particularly the French) who, after simply breathing the free air of America, had repudiated old truths and embraced their new land with the passion of despair – but without writing about it. The Amerindians did not write either, and the takeover of America by Europe's churches and states seemed easy enough to accomplish until the day when a literate brother of the savages, Lahontan, that implacable apostate, arrived with his pen. "I have passed the finest days of my life with the Savages of America," the author declared in his dedication to the king of Denmark of *Mémoires de l'Amérique septentrionale*.

LAHONTAN'S SELF-DEFENCE

Despite all the attempts to cast doubt on him, Lahontan remains a cultivated seventeenth-century European who conducted an intelligent trial of two opposing civilizations, from which the Amerindians emerged victorious. It is important to know that Lahontan's observations date from the most troubled period in the development of New France, a time when other observers created the negative image of the Amerindian that still does so much harm.

As we have seen, Lahontan had some very strong and honourable defenders. But he also defended himself against his numerous and influential detractors, who included of course the journalists of Trévoux – that is, the Jesuits.

To those Jesuits who said of him that "it would be not so grave were he but a bad Writer, but he is also a dangerous Author,"[6] Lahontan retorted: "[Many *Relations* have already been given] to the public, but all have one essential flaw, a lack of selflessness and sincerity. The Authors are Missionaries, that is individuals whose profession engages them to persuade people that their pains, which to be sure are praiseworthy, are not altogether fruitless. That is why their narrations are, strictly speaking, merely a detailed account of Masses, miracles, conversions, and other downright fraudulent trifling details which hardly agree with the good sense of our time; in a word, these Authors, driven by a false or genuine zeal, have written more for the credit of their cause than to give the reader the genuine contents of what goes on in those countries."[7]

The baron replied even more vehemently when the same Jesuits declared him to be nothing but a superficial "maker of relations."[8] His response: "The ways that are used to gain more credence for the Apostles in question are most subtle. They have, it is said, converted thousands of *Canadois* [Amerindians]; they have performed miracles among these people who have made martyrs of them for their faith, and Fathers Brébeuf and l'Alleman are said to have been burned by slow fire by the Yroquois, not for their faith but because they were convinced they were the driving force behind the war then being waged on these people."[9] And when attempts were made to cast doubt on his religious convictions, Lahontan questioned even the faith of the Jesuits themselves: "I doubt that the Gentlemen Journalists be as good Catholics as I: should that be the case they would not dare to divide heaven between Confucius and Jesus Christ, nor to give communion to peoples who do not believe in the Incarnation."[10]

The Jesuits, who ingenuously acknowledged their imperialistic background, finally observed about the baron that "if he were engaged in America only in 'discovering' new lands, no doubt he would not have drawn the indignation of the Court, of which he now complains."[11] In his own defence, Lahontan shows that, like his Amerindian intellectual and spiritual guides, he was not the enemy of any state or religion, but rather of that same imperialistic thinking: "If the Clergy were only busy serving God; if they did not meddle in the affairs of Princes and individuals; and if they did not make it their law to have absolute authority over the minds of all, they would not incur so many reproaches. I have only observed that those who most flatter them are the ones who most fear them."[12]

ADARIO: THE WENDAT WHO REVOLUTIONIZED THE WORLD

It was Lahontan's adoptive brothers the Amerindians, however, who were his main defenders, providing him with the bulk of his arguments and thus his ideas. It is undeniable that he lived intimately with the Amerindians, especially the Algonkins. It is even certain that the Jesuits scorned him for that: "The Baron de La Hontan has been so long among the Canadois that he may well have taken on some of their inclinations."[13] The baron was flattered by this remark: "It is the best thing that the Journalists have said in their extract; for I have found such charm in the amiable freedom of the Canadois, and such cruelty in my slavery, that there is no difference between the Natives' soul and my own."[14]

In a letter, he refers proudly to the intellectual level of his adoptive society: "The fact remains that their Lordships le Comte de Frontenac, le Marquis de Seignelay and de la Barre, who would surely rank at the head of people of wit and good taste [in New France] have admired a hundred times both the soundness of the arguments and the reasoning power of these naked Philosophers."[15] Among those Amerindian thinkers it was a Wendat chief of the Turtle Clan, named Kondiaronk, who would best incarnate for Lahontan the physical, moral, and intellectual qualities of the first Americans.

The French called Kondiaronk "the Rat," in the same way that they gave his people, the Wendat, the humiliating name "Hurons" (meaning unkempt and barbaric) because of their compulsive need to disparage anything they recognized as proud. Among his own people, Kondiaronk was also known as Adario, meaning great and noble friend. In Lahontan's book *Dialogues curieux entre l'auteur et un Sauvage de bon sens qui a voyagé*, he takes on the aspect of a philosopher.

For the Wendat, Adario simultaneously assumed the functions of chief of "war" (we would say external affairs), and council chief. All historians, even those least inclined to admiration of Adario, have recognized the great refinement of his political thought, as well as the uncommonly keen intelligence which made him stand out even among the European élite. "He was no less brilliant in private conversations," Charlevoix reports, "and we often took pleasure in irritating him so as to hear his retorts, which were always lively, full of wit, and generally irrefutable. On that score, he was the only man in Canada able to stand up to the Comte de Frontenac, who often invited him to his table to procure this pleasure to his officers."[16] As for Adario, he would say that "among the French he knew only two men of wit and learning, Governor Frontenac and the Jesuit priest Carheil."[17] The latter was the friend and confessor of the chief, who was baptized shortly before his death in 1701.

Lahontan belonged to the inner circle of Frontenac, called by the pro-Jesuit faction of the colony "an old fox who cared about nothing except protecting vice."[18] In his preface to the 1703 edition of the *Dialogues*, Lahontan refers to his closeness to the Wendat chief, and to the latter's friendship with the governor of the colony: "I made it my agreeable duty when I was in this American's village to carefully take note of all his arguments. No sooner was I home from my journey to the lakes of Canada when I showed my manuscript to Monsieur le Comte de Frontenac, who was so delighted to read it that he afterwards took the trouble to help me put these Dialogues into their present state."[19]

The most serious accusation against Lahontan's work to date is that he had fabricated his *Dialogues* from unverifiable remarks by a man unable to appreciate a civilized society – in other words a savage. The Québécois historian J-.Edmond Roy wrote in 1903: "The great error Lahontan committed in these dialogues is to have attributed to the Savages refined ideas and subtle feelings, and to have expressed opinions that disagree with the established order of things among civilized nations."[20] Yet Charlevoix does say about Lahontan's philosophical ally that "it was the general sentiment that never has a Savage had more merit, a finer genius, more valour, more prudence, or more judgment."[21]

Besides, who today would still maintain that the Amerindians of Lahontan's time were incapable of analysis or reason? It is important to see that it is not Lahontan's thinking that is being repudiated, but the Amerindian's revolt; rejecting the pro-Amerindian philosophical argument of one of the Europeans who knew them best is equivalent to denying the Amerindian himself.

In any event, Lahontan's and Adario's analysis carried them much beyond a simple trial of the two civilizations: using their knowledge of European society and their discoveries about American society, they produced a new treatise on human nature.

Henceforth it would be impossible to talk about humans as beings who possessed a uniform and universal vision and destiny. The Amerindian Adario and his interpreter, Lahontan, changed the meaning of all the big words: religion, society, man, woman, nature ...

Data gathered through our autohistorical analysis confirm that Lahontan has passed on, not only a reliable translation of the feelings of the voiceless Amerindian people, but also an unusually accurate picture of aboriginal American ideology.

Obviously, the elaboration of the ideas in the *Dialogues* could have been accomplished only by a young European who had transformed himself, through desire and necessity, into the American air and essence, and moulded himself into the spirit of America's original inhabitants. "Ah!" exclaims Adario, "long live the Hurons who, without laws or prisons or tortures, spend their lives in sweet tranquility and enjoy happiness unknown to the French. We live simply, following the laws of instinct and innocent conduct with which Nature in its wisdom has marked us from the cradle."[22] Adario says, in effect, that the language of nature is the sole authentic message from God, because of its dazzling, universal clarity. It alone can rally all humans, if only they will listen. That is why Adario's message (although extremely categorical), through his interpreter, Lahontan, has echoed so profoundly in the hearts of other peoples.

Lahontan summed up his philosophical ideas in the *Dialogues*, presented in five chapters, each dealing with a major aspect of the human condition: religion, laws, happiness, medicine and health, and, finally, love and marriage.[23]

RELIGION

Adario notes that religion is a cause of discord and confusion. Amerindian wisdom does not try to know or explain "what happens in the other World." Agreeing with the notion of the "vision" which is specific to each individual, the Wendat chief suggests that "the Great Spirit has given us the power to reason and to know Good, which is as far removed from Evil as Heaven is from Earth, so that we may observe the Rules of Justice and Wisdom. The Great Master of Life wants our Souls to be tranquil and at peace; he abhors turmoil and a troubled mind, for that is what makes Men wicked."[24]

As to the truth of Revelation, Lahontan found that Amerindian society confirmed and justified the skepticism characteristic of his time. Adario says: "To be enlightened by those holy Scriptures you and your Jesuits are endlessly quoting to us, it is first necessary to have this blind Faith with which the good Fathers stun us at every moment ... You will never make me conceive that one can believe something without first seeing it with his own eyes, or without its being proven through clear and solid truths already known to us."[25]

Elsewhere, Lahontan states even more clearly how the Amerindian cultural trait of "Believe what you see"[26] transformed his own personal doubt into certainty, allowing him to see how fundamentally unfair were the imperialistic ideas of people who claimed to be Christians. "Let us all unanimously admire the greatness of Divine Providence which authorizes these nations to turn away *quickly*, as can be seen, from that which we hold sacred, and which allows us to progress and to surpass them independently of our merit."[27]

Adario's argument about the obscurity of the message of Jesus Christ – the cause of so many misunderstandings and wars between individuals and societies – basically concurs with the teachings of contemporary Mohawk artist and historian Louis Hall Karaniaktajeh: "The missionaries say they brought God to America. Helpless God. Can't go anywhere by himself. Needs the missionaries to take him here and there. They still say they're bringing God to the jungles in South America and Africa."[28] Adario continues: "If [on the contrary] what you call the Gospel truly comes from him, we must conclude that God has spoken in this world only to stir up Troubles and Divisions, which is incompatible with his Goodness."[29]

Adario concludes his argument with the baron with a thought that would contribute to Lahontan's condemnation by his own society – just as that same society condemned the Amerindian: "The Great Spirit is wise, all his Works are perfect, it is he who has made us and he alone knows what will become of us. It is therefore up to us to live in peace, without worrying about what we cannot understand. He has willed you to be born in France so that your eyes and your Reason be of no use to you. He has made me be born Huron and believe only what I can see and understand."[30]

Revealing the vocation of America to the Europeans, Lahontan, through Adario's voice, declares that he is convinced "that we Hurons are the works and creations of the Great Spirit, that he made us good and without malice, whereas you are villains brought to this Land by Providence so that you may correct yourselves through our example and imitate the uprightness and simplicity of our ways."[31] At the end of this chapter, Adario states the credo of which he certainly taught a good part to his brother, Lahontan:

So, my brother, believe what you will, have as much faith as it pleases you, you will never go to the Good Land of Souls unless you become a Huron. The innocence of our life, the love we have for one another, the tranquillity of soul which we enjoy because we scorn self-interest are three things the Great Spirit requires of all men in general. We practise them naturally in our villages, while the Europeans tear each other apart, rob, defame and kill one another in their cities, they who wishing to go to the Land of Souls, think about their Creator only when they talk about Him with the Hurons.[32]

LAWS

The tone of the *Dialogues* becomes noticeably more personal and passionate when Lahontan starts to consider the laws of his society. The injustice and humiliation he suffered at the hands of lawyers and jurists in his native country sometimes mar the philosophical objective of his message. All the main points he raises, however, clearly correspond to the essential and durable Amerindian values noted in the course of our autohistorical analysis.

First, with remarkable perspicacity for his time, Lahontan knew, associated with, and above all appreciated Amerindians enough to recognize the universality of their pacifist thought. As one of his contemporaries noted, "[The baron] praises enough the humanity of the savage nations through which he was obliged to pass. They do not wage war out of ferocity or for pillaging; they do so only when it is necessary for their own defence. Thus

M. le Baron de La Hontan, who had no orders either to attack them or to conquer them, went very far without encountering any other obstacles than the inconveniences of the journey. He first displayed the Great Calumet, that is the great Pipe which is a sacred and inviolable sign of friendship and peace."[33]

In the *Dialogues* Adario, like all Amerindians of all times, insists upon his people's sovereignty before the Great Spirit, the only being to whom all humans must answer for their acts: "Let us now come to these laws or reasonable things. For fifty years, the governors of Canada claimed that we were under the laws of their great Captain. We for our part merely deny that we are subordinate to anyone but the Great Spirit. We are born free and united brothers, each as great a master as the other, whereas you are all slaves of only one man ... Upon what rights and what authority do they base this claim? Have we sold ourselves to that great Captain? Did we go to France to look for you? It is you who came here to us. Who has given you all the lands you now inhabit? By what right do you own them? They belong to the [Amerindians] from time immemorial."[34] Is this not the identical judgment of any Amerindian today?

In his comparative analysis of the two societies, Adario agrees with Lafitau's Iroquois who, a generation later, were shocked that Europeans should have enemies among their own nations: "Oh what a fine man is the Frenchman with all his laws who, believing himself very wise, is most assuredly foolish, since he lives in slavery and dependence while the very animals enjoy the delights of freedom and, like ourselves, fear only *foreign* enemies."[35]

By denouncing the European judicial system, Lahontan shows himself to be quite aware of imperialistic attitudes towards the "savage," proving not only his unusual mental acuity but uncommon honesty as well. His presentation of Adario's opinions make his work a reliable Amerindian source. When the baron objects, for example, that French judges are universally honest ("bad ones, one could not perhaps find more than four in all of France"[36]), Adario replies that he had learned of "a peasant who was to be whipped for having taken partridges and hares with snares." Adario's reflection, which follows, in our opinion gives irrefutable proof of Lahontan's ability to see through Amerindian eyes and, therefore, of the pertinence and honesty of his testimony: "Where then are those fair and reasonable laws, where are those judges who have a soul as do you and I? After this, you still dare to say that the Hurons are beasts? Truly, it would be a fine affair if we were to punish one of our brothers for some hares and partridges!"[37] Here, Lahontan goes considerably beyond the bounds of his subject; why, in fact, is it inconceivable that someone in America should be punished for taking hares and partridges when the Amerindians still controlled the Department of Wildlife and Flora? It is conservation that Lahontan is discussing here, and ecology. Who besides the Amerindians was aware of this social dimension in the eighteenth century? And what is the source of Lahontan's uncommon understanding?

The chapter on laws ends with Adario's advice to Lahontan on the European notion of private property, the source of so many social ills from which the Amerindians, believers in "neither thine nor mine," are exempt:

> Reason is our sole and Sovereign Judge: it commands us to make one another happy, and to work towards the common happiness by sharing goods equally, and we obey it rigorously: it further commands us to work for abundance and security within the Village, which we do most willingly. What occurs then? Banishing thus from our midst the notions of Mine and Thine, those two great Disturbers of the World, we live a life exempt from ambition and dispute and, in consequence, we enjoy an unshakeable and unalterable felicity.[38]

HAPPINESS

Even more than the other parts of his work, Lahontan's discussion with Adario about happiness underlines the fact that Amerindians of all times feel perfectly at ease with their value system.

To his European and imperialist interlocutor who tells him that he has "no other interest but that of showing [him] the happiness of the French, so that he may live like them, along with the rest of his nation,"[39] the Wendat chief gives the logical Amerindian answer: "We have talked about religion and laws; my answers have been only a quarter of what I really thought about all the reasons which you put forward. You rebuke our way of living, the French in general take us for beasts, the Jesuits call us impious, fools, ignorant, and vagabonds, and we look at all of you in the same way. With this difference, that we are content to pity you without insulting you."[40] Later, regarding the Amerindians' attachment to their land, Adario observes: "We are not given to leave our country, of which we know, as you are aware, the smallest little stream up to four hundred leagues around."[41]

In this chapter, the "two authors" of the *Dialogues* examine and condemn:

- Money. "Wanting to live in lands of money and preserve one's soul, is like wanting to throw oneself to the bottom of a lake to preserve one's life … For money is the father … of all the evils that are in the world."[42]
- Blind, imperialistic faith in technology. "You say, finally, that the French save us from misery out of pity for us. And *how did our Ancestors manage one hundred years ago*? If our Fathers have done without all those goods for so many centuries, I believe we could do without them *more easily than the French without our beavers*, in exchange for which, in good friendship, they give us rifles that maim us … axes that break … knives that lose their edge by cutting a pumpkin … And that, my brother," Adario concludes, "is what I have to say to you about the woes of the Hurons."[43]
- Wealth. By contrasting the happiness of "the only happy Frenchman, the king" with the well-being of the Wendat who "even though naked have a contented soul," Adario answers the baron's question: "Is there in the world any life more pleasant and delectable than that of an infinite number of rich people who lack for nothing?"[44]
- Ambition, source of imbalance between body and spirit. "Tell me, I pray," Adario asks the baron, "is it not necessary, if one is to enjoy good health, that the body work and the mind rest? and conversely, to destroy one's health, that the body rest while the mind is active?"[45] He adds that one should enjoy life, the only true wealth we possess. "The French destroy their health in a thousand different ways, while we preserve ours until our bodies are used up, for our souls, devoid of passions, can neither alter nor trouble our bodies. Believe me, my dear brother, consider becoming Huron if you would live a long life."[46]
- Strong drink and food. "What purposes are served," asks Adario, "by salt, pepper, and a thousand other spices, except to ruin the health? … Wine and brandy destroy the body's natural

warmth, debilitate the stomach, burn the blood, intoxicate, and cause a thousand disorders."[47]

- Europeans' unhealthy clothing, their servile and affected language, their feigned sociability, the widespread servitude of the weak.
- Writing as a source of numerous misfortunes. "Every day," observes Adario, "I see a thousand quarrels here between the *coureurs de bois* ... It takes but one piece of paper ... to ruin a family." Adario and his adoptive brother conclude, referring to the "histories of Canada": "Horrible lies and impertinences are written in books every day, and you would have me know how to read and write like the French? No, my brother, I would rather live without knowing it."[48]

Lahontan ends this discussion about happiness by affirming the unique and independent nature of the Native American's ideological and philosophical system, and in so doing he once again demonstrates his right to the title of discover of Americity: "We have seen in France," says the offended baron, "Chinese and Siamese, people from the other end of the world, who are in every respect more opposed to our manners than the Huron, yet they have unflagging admiration for our way of living. As for me, I admit that I do not comprehend your obstinacy."[49] "All those people," Adario answers him, "have between them the notion of 'Thine and Mine,' as do the French; they use money as well as the French ... It is not upon those people that the Hurons will model themselves." Adario ends condescendingly: "You should not be offended by what I have proven to you, and I do not despise the Europeans in their presence, I merely pity them."[50]

MEDICINE AND HEALTH

The Americized Lahontan may have been the first European (and that is one more proof of his authenticity) who felt the need to convince Western society of the benefits of a natural life. One of his many reflections, as reported by a contemporary, has to do with the importance of being aware of what one eats:

The air of the country [Denmark] is very healthy for sober people and very contrary for those whose minds are not content. Almost no disease is known there apart from Scurvy. The Physicians attribute the cause to the salt air laden with an infinity of thick, condensed vapours, which come together close to the Earth's surface, seep along with air into the lungs and, mixing with the blood, so much delay its movement that it coagulates, thereby giving rise to all the symptoms of Scurvy. This is not the opinion of Mr de La Hontan, he believes [and modern medical opinion concurs] that the air's impressions upon the blood mass are less strong than those of food. He maintains that if Scurvy were caused by the bad qualities of the air, it would follow that everyone would be attacked by it, and yet three quarters of all Danes are exempt. It is really food, then, that causes this disease, that is salted meats, butter, and cheese. To them must be added lack of exercise and immoderate sleeping.[51]

Medical science today shows that scurvy, which was unknown to the Amerindians, is directly attributable to a diet deficient in Vitamin C. We know as well that the characteristic unhealthiness of Old World cities was responsible for the tainted air that was breathed there. Amerindians, in contrast, were aware of the laws of movement and periodically changed the sites of their villages, mainly to allow Nature to "remake itself" and to plan ecological zones where their wild "cattle" could find abundant pastureland. By so doing, they ensured the salubrity of the space reserved for humans.

In the chapter on medicine, Lahontan has trouble finding matters on which to disagree with Adario. In view of the great longevity of some Amerindians, he acknowledges the relationship between health and physical activity that Adario had noted. Similarly, Lahontan has to admit that the efficiency of a defence force depends far more on the combatants' physical fitness than on any bookish knowledge of battle.

Adario (the speaker here is obviously Lahontan), repeats what all Europeans without exception had noted, two hundred years after contact, when Amerindians *still* possessed the admirable physical attributes of their race:

Our temperaments and our complexions are as different from yours as night from day. And this great difference which I notice in all things between the Europeans and the peoples of Canada would almost persuade me that we are not descended from your so-called Adam. For one thing there are among us hardly any who are hunchbacks, cripples, dwarfs, deaf, mute, blind from birth, to say nothing of one-eyed ... As for diseases, we never see dropsy, asthma, paralysis, gout, or pox; we have no leprosy, sores, tumors, retention of urine, stones, or gravel, to the astonishment of the French who are so prone to those ills.[52]

Continuing his lesson in preventive medicine, the Wendat chief again impresses upon his friend the beneficial effects on health of a calm, simple life, free of ambition and worries, and above all, of the anger and anxiety that so often accompany thwarted plans. Similarly, he insists that Europeans would do well to abstain from spicy food and drink.

Denys Delâge notes that in European cities, water – which was contaminated – was the drink of the poor; the well-to-do drank wine. To the Jesuits and other Europeans, the Amerindians, who drank only pure water and plain broths, deserved pity, if not contempt.

The Amerindians' sexual moderation was another point that struck Lahontan, one he emphasized several times in his three main books. He maintained that Europeans, lacking sufficient control over the passions, lost their vitality much earlier in life than did the Amerindians, for whom reason must always prevail: "Our [unmarried] daughters," Adario recounts, "admit that the French are older in this [sexual] commerce at the age of thirty-five than our Hurons are at fifty. This admission ... led me to reflect that ... those illnesses we talked about are no doubt the result of those immoderate pleasures, and also of the time and manner in which you take them. For when you have completed a meal or an exhausting day of work, you embrace your women."[53]

Central to Amerindian medicine was the sweat-lodge, and Lahontan obviously knew its benefits, making him a heretic as far as the "advanced" medicine of his time was concerned. Always in the vanguard, he knew that the racism of European and Euroamerican doctors kept them from recognizing the natural medicine of Native people, particularly the sweat-lodge, and he did not hesitate to offer his own medical opinion, quoting Adario:

"The fact remains that if, from time to time, you wish to sweat in this manner, you will be as fit as possible and whatever evil humours that wine, spices, excesses of women [*sic*] have engendered in your blood will emerge through the pores of your flesh. And then, farewell to medicine and all its poisons! Now what I am telling you, dear brother, is clearer than the day; this reasoning is not for the ignorant."[54] Lahontan, who had obviously assimilated his Amerindian friend's lessons, adds Adario's comments: "The fact remains, my dear brother, that Nature is a good mother who would have us live eternally. However, so violently do we torment her that she is sometimes so weakened she barely has the strength to bring us sustenance."[55]

LOVE AND MARRIAGE

Aside from cannibalism, it was probably for their sexual freedom that Amerindians were most condemned by European "converters" of all types. Of all the early European chroniclers, Lahontan provides the best information on how Amerindians perceived their sexual morality. Because he avoided the places where missionaries were insouciantly reorganizing the consciences of their converts, he stayed in contact with Amerindians who were closer to their traditions. As an educated *coureur de bois* as well as a close friend of the great Adario and of so many other "naked philosophers," he made a genuine effort to defend the integrity of Amerindian culture on a number of essential points.

First, he established a fundamental cultural trait: the Amerindian woman is under no one's control. She marries whom she wants, when she wants, *if* she wants. From puberty, she freely follows the course that nature has imparted to her, and it is she who controls the sexual relation. A child born to an unmarried mother will bear her name and belong to her and her clan; and she may choose the "official" father from among the men who may claim to have engendered her child. Because of the tremendous importance attached to the human being in their value system, Amerindian women welcomed children with the utmost gratitude, manifesting admirable patience and affection. However, should a pregnancy be undesired or considered by the medicine women to be dangerous to the mother's health, an abortion could be induced by means of abortifacient plants or various techniques, and no one judged this as being wrong. Furthermore, it was rare for a woman to have more than four children.

After marriage, the sexual freedom of young Amerindians was transformed into exemplary fidelity. "I am convinced," Lahontan wrote in his *Mémoires*, "that a Savage would sooner suffer mutilation than caress his neighbour's wife. The chastity of Savage women is no less strict."[56] Among Europeans, in contrast, the man possesses mysterious but real rights over the woman, and is less bound to fidelity than she is. The men do their utmost to "tempt girls and women. They use all sorts of means to succeed in this. And then they make public the fact, they tell it everywhere. Everyone praises the cavalier and despises the lady, instead of forgiving the lady and punishing the cavalier." How, asks Adario, "can you pretend that your women are faithful to you if you are not faithful to them?"[57]

Later, Adario states that his people, "savage" though they may be, "are unacquainted with the kind of misery that inspires civilized men to sell their women ... The Huron are greatly fortunate that they are not reduced to committing the despicable acts which misery inspires in people who are not accustomed to being miserable. We are never either rich or poor; and for that reason our happiness is beyond all your wealth."[58]

The nakedness of Amerindian men in hot weather is the mark of a society where all are equal because, according to Adario, "it is by their clothing that [Europeans] assess the rank of others."[59] Nudity is also proof of an honest mind and the prerogative of a body that has nothing to hide. "Is it not a great advantage for a Frenchman to be able to hide some natural defect under fine clothes? ... Girls seeing young men naked can judge with their own eyes what suits them. Nature has made no more allowances for women than for men ... That is all I can tell you about the crime of nudity which, as you know, must only be attributed to the boys ... Besides, our girls are more modest than yours, for the only part of them that we see naked is the fleshy part of the leg."[60]

Among Amerindians, as the two fellow-philosophers note, love is the only grounds for marriage. Similarly, if love ends, couples separate, and should they remarry, that too is done out of love, never self-interest, in this society where "no one wants to handle or even to see" money, the "serpent of the French."[61]

Finally, Lahontan and Adario declare proudly that, in "their" society, virginity is not prized, any more than prolonged continence. Nor does the European style of courtship, with all its assiduous attentions, its gallantry, and its respectful, endless waiting, stir their admiration. Lahontan was now so steeped in the spirit of his adoptive people that, through Adario, he denied his very homeland: "I have been so foolish as to risk my life on impertinent ships, crossing the rough seas which separate France from this continent, for the pleasure of seeing the land of the French. Which obliges me to keep my mouth shut."[62]

After talking about unreasonable love affairs, Lahontan ends his book, the discussion, and, symbolically, his life as a European by giving the last word to Adario: "But reasonable people will say that these kinds of lovers are as mad as I, the difference being that their love goes blindly from one mistress to another, exposing them to the same torments, whereas I will not in all my life pass again from America to France.[63]

CONCLUSION

Religious doubt was in fashion when Lahontan was born in 1666, and a taste for liberation and anarchy hung over Europe. Many great minds had already drawn revolutionary conclusions from the accounts circulating about the New World, and constructed daring theories aimed at overthrowing feudal systems, particularly in France, which lagged behind its colonial competitors, especially Holland.

So far, however, no one had shown how American Natives themselves saw their world, in comparison with the old one. To explain how the philosophical system of this "new human being" functioned was the lot of the Baron de Lahontan, who would certainly have been only a fairly ordinary writer in Europe had not his family's financial reverses uprooted him and driven him to America. There he befriended Adario and numerous other "naked philosophers" who helped make him into a thinker who would have an impact on the course of Western civilization. As one of his biographers has put it, "The pendulum of Lahontan's life had more than once swung between solitude and society, between Europe and North America. As a youthful subject of Louis XIV he had left the Old World for the New; as an early writer of the Enlightenment, he brought the New World to the Old."[64]

Lahontan became too Americized to be able to continue living in Europe. In addition, his writing, especially in his native France, had brought him the widespread contempt of the authorities. Even the greatest thinkers, who were abundantly inspired by him, almost never dared to quote him. "How many more philosophers of the eighteenth century have drawn from him without letting it show?" J.-Edmond Roy has asked. "They have not deemed it convenient to tell posterity from what dungheap of Ennius they were gathering pearls."[65]

The authenticity of Adario was denied by almost everyone, particularly the Jesuits: "The objections which he has the Savages state against the Religion that our missionaries announced to them are liable to impress mediocre minds." Lahontan retorts: "How will the Journalists prove that I put objections in the Savages' mouths? I am sure that those Doctors know the Hurons too well to doubt that they raise much more extravagant or ridiculous objections than the ones I have mentioned."[66]

"A strange destiny," observes Réal Ouellet, "is that of Lahontan, for we know neither the place nor the date of his death. The writer who without a doubt has best crystallized the myth of the happy primitive, stranger to the notion of Thine and Mine, having neither priests nor laws, disappeared like his Savages, whose death leaves no trace in the archives."[67] For having championed the Amerindian vision of life in his writing, Lahontan was indeed despised, dispossessed, a thousand times accused, denied, banished, but he was never forgotten. Indeed, his work, because of a humanity as strange as it was real, as profound as it was new, has gained immortality. As for the author himself, steeped in the truth that he found and revealed in the face of all opposition, he quietly turned his back on incomprehension and persecution, trusting in the safety of his simple refuge:

What road shall I then follow to extract myself from the Labyrinth in which I find myself? I see none that is surer than America, where I shall have the pleasure of living at rest among peoples less savage than we: in that they are not reduced to the fatal necessity to bend the knee before certain demi-gods whom we worship under the fine name of Ministers of State ... who will always be right until Anarchy be introduced among us as it exists among the Americans, who filled with the charity of St. Paul, will never envy us "et Meum et Tuum".[68]

Like all great visionaries, Lahontan was hated and humiliated. Through his writing, he imparted to the world one of the greatest ideas in its history: the Native American political idea of *a world without countries or religions*. In his dedication of the *Mémoires* to the king of Denmark, he wrote: "The author has applied himself only to presenting things simply; he flatters no one, he disguises nothing, and one could rightly attribute to him the qualities needed by any good narrator, to write as if he had neither Country nor Religion."[69]

The Baron de Lahontan and the Wendat Adario had already foreseen the need for a world government and may be said to have helped lay the intellectual foundations for the great social revolutions of our own time. For the purposes of our autohistorical analysis, the two constitute an invaluable Amerindian source.

CHAPTER 6

THE DISPERSAL OF THE WENDAT

In 1982 the province of Quebec instituted legal proceedings against four individuals (including this writer) of the Wendat nation (today known as the Huron-Wendat nation) for having engaged in some of their people's traditional activities on territories where they possessed ancestral rights. The province, denying Native rights over the territories concerned, attempted to define the Wendat as immigrants on Quebec soil (see appendix).

The Wendat saw this as an opportunity to establish the nature of their rights on Quebec territory. Among other points, they had to prove that the Wendat who took refuge in Quebec in 1650 – whose descendants are the Wendat of Lorette – were ethnically related to the St Lawrence Iroquoians. After Jacques Cartier's visit, these people mysteriously disappeared from the regions of "Quebec" that had been their country from time immemorial and that comprised the lands traditionally occupied and claimed by the Wendat of Lorette.

I believe that the autohistorical approach may help safeguard the right of an Amerindian group to territories denied it by traditional non-Amerindian history.

THE WENDAT BEFORE 1649[1]

The Laurentian Nadoueks in Cartier's Time

Modern professional historians have given the name St Lawrence

Iroquoians to the non-Algonquian peoples who inhabited the Laurentian region upriver from Île aux Coudres at the time of Cartier. In the light of recent archaeological findings, as well as linguistics and Amerindian oral tradition, I believe that just as the Iroquois were, to a large extent, unfairly blamed for the seventeenth-century dispersal of the Wendat, so has the designation "Iroquoians" helped establish official theories aimed at eliminating from Quebec the reality and rights of the Wendat. I shall use instead the term "Laurentian Nadoueks" – Nadoueks being the name given by many Algonquian tribes to all peoples of "Iroquian" stock.[1]

The Laurentian Nadoueks at Champlain's Arrival

When Champlain arrived, some seventy years after Cartier, all of the fifteen or twenty ancient villages had disappeared. Historians and archaeologists generally agree that the coming of Europeans caused major upheavals in the political and cultural order maintained by Native nations until then. Most recent serious studies (for example, the one by the American demographer Henry F. Dobyns) support the suggestion that European epidemic diseases were the determining factor in these disruptions, the one that best explains their magnitude. Add to that scourge the kidnappings, skirmishes between the two cultural groups, intensification of conflicts between Native nations, and other disorders, and the disappearance of the Laurentian Nadoueks is easily explained. In my opinion, the survivors of that dispersal then sought and found refuge principally among the Wendat of Huronia, and their Wendat descendants were dispersed *for the second time* during the 1640s, still because of European epidemic diseases, of which the Iroquois wars were but a consequence.

The Archaeological Evidence

In 1978, archaeologist James A. Tuck wrote in the *Handbook of North American Indians*:

> A series of local and sometimes culturally distinguishable developments seem to have taken place from Middle Woodland times until the early to mid-sixteenth century when the entire sequence was truncated. The

reasons are not demonstrable but perhaps include disease, conflict with the Five Nations, or some other decimation related to the coming of the Europeans, whose presence was being increasingly felt in the St. Lawrence Valley. Occasional traces of their material cultures show up in Onondaga about 1550 but the main destination of refugees seems most likely to have been Huronia.[2]

In a recent interview, the distinguished anthropologist, ethnohistorian, and Wendat specialist, Bruce G. Trigger, formulated the hypothesis of an exodus of the Laurentians to Huronia, a theory now confirmed by archaeology. According to Trigger, most survivors of the Laurentian Nadoueks merged with the nations of Huronia. In fact, vestiges of their material culture – mainly pottery – have been found on every Wendat site excavated. The Wendat of Lorette, Trigger concludes, form the only historic "Iroquoian" group that can claim at this point to be the rightful heirs, ethnic and territorial, of the Laurentian Nadoueks.

On the other hand, James F. Pendergast, the distinguished Ontario specialist in Nadouek archaeology, declared in a personal communication that the numerous pottery fragments found among the Montagnais of mid-northern Quebec (especially in the Lac Saint-Jean basin) and the Mistassini Cree, which until recently were thought to be of Wendat origin, were actually made by these Algonquian peoples, indicating Wendat cultural influence. This Wendat cultural "presence" so far from their own territory is a solid indication, according to Pendergast, of cultural exchange and harmony between peoples otherwise very distinct, and it sheds new and interesting light on the nature of pre-contact northeast Amerindian geo-politics. In addition, new knowledge about these communities supports the notion of a cultural relationship between the Wendats of Ontario and the Stadaconans of Quebec, who were commercial and most certainly cultural partners of the politically interrelated Algonquian peoples, among whom the historical "Hurons" already had territorial and political bases in 1649.

The Ethnohistorical Evidence

The Laurentian Nadoueks' migration to Huronia can also be explained through cultural kinship. All evidence (archaeological, ethnographic, linguistic, and so on) indicates that the cultural essence of the vast majority of the Nadoueks was manifested through trade and exchange, both among themselves and with their numerous Algonquian neighbours, as well as with Siouan groups and possibly others. The first Nadoueks were located at the crossroads of the commercial networks. This was especially true for the two groups under discussion here – the Wendat of Huronia and the Stadaconans, or the original inhabitants of the "Province of Canada," of which Stadacona (Quebec) was the capital. Because of remarkable cultural complementarity, the Stadaconans, along with the Wendat and Algonquians from regions farther north, formed symbiotic communities. While they belonged to very dissimilar races, these Amerindians had no segregationist or exclusivist territorial or cultural policies towards one another. As Trigger notes:

From the beginnings of horticulture in this area, they [the Wendat] appear to have traded corn, tobacco, fishing nets, and other products of southern Ontario for the skins and dried fish and meat that were produced by the hunting and gathering peoples who lived to the north. This symbiotic exchange was beneficial to both groups and probably supported a denser population on both sides of this ecological boundary than would have been possible otherwise. There is some evidence that a similar trade may have gone on between the Iroquoian tribes in the upper Saint Lawrence Valley and the Algonquins and Montagnais who lived north of them.[3]

The Jesuits and Recollets report that the Wendat language was the *lingua franca* of some fifty nations who had political and trading ties among themselves and with the Wendat. In 1632, Recollet brother Gabriel Sagard-Théodat published a Wendat dictionary for the benefit of those who:

desire to go to the country for the conversion of the Savages, or otherwise to settle there and live as Christians. Our dictionary shall teach them all things principal and necessary that they shall have to say to the Hurons and to the other Provinces and Nations among whom that language is in use, such as the Petuns [Tobacco], the Neutral Nation, the Province of Fire, that of the Winnebago, the Nation of the Woods, that of the Copper Mine, the Iroquois, the Province of the Raised-Up-Hair

[Nipissing], and many others. Then the Nation of the Sorcerers, those of the Island [Manitoulin], the Small Nation, and the Algonquins, who know it in part for the need they have of it when they travel or when they have to deal with people of our Huron and Sedentary provinces.[4]

As for the Native "Canada" of Cartier's time, it consisted of a dozen villages and hamlets, none of them palisaded, which informs us as to the state of relations between the Wendat-Iroquoians and their Algonquian neighbours, with whom they had long since established the custom of trading.

Wendats and Stadaconans (we refer to them because it was in the town of Quebec that the historical "Hurons" decided to relocate, in 1649) were thus commercial partners of the ethnically and politically interrelated Algonquian peoples. After Cartier, when the decimated Laurentian Nadoueks (among them the Stadaconans) withdrew among the Wendat of Huronia in Ontario, their former Algonquian partners became the only Amerindians to occupy, albeit sporadically, these former lands of sedentary peoples. When the epidemics of 1630–50 brought about a second dispersal, however, this time in Huronia, part of the Wendat, that is the historic "Huron," went back and occupied territories along the St Lawrence. An absence of three generations had not been long enough to dissolve the very solid political and interethnic ties that had melded the two races into one. The "Huron," returning to live among their own relatives after their dispersal, obviously did not have to ask permission of their Algonquian brothers to occupy and live off territories they had always shared. The testimonies of elders, mostly Montagnais, Algonquian, and Wendat, still attest to their amiable relations, and always refer to their "brotherhood."

Huronia, the Heartland, and the Extended Wendat Society

The ancestors of the Wendat of Lorette cultivated many varieties of beans, corn, and squash, and traded their surpluses with the Algonquian nations that lived in their vicinity. Wendat food products were so important to the hunting nations that the French referred to the Wendat country as "the Algonquins' granary."

Some nations were even in the habit of wintering near the Wendat nations, creating cross-cultural customs that have persisted in certain forms until today. Trigger reports that "in Jesuit times groups numbering several hundred each would come each year to trade for corn and would pass the winter near the Huron villages."[5] And William N. Fenton writes that "in the process of raising on the order of 189,000 bushels of corn per year, the 21,000 Hurons had cleared and cultivated close to 7000 acres of land."[6] Geographer and historian Conrad E. Heidenreich tells us that "Champlain and other French writers claimed that Huronia was for the most part cleared. Huronia was described as a country 'full of fine hills, open fields, very beautiful broad meadows bearing much excellent hay.' The numerous statements regarding grass-covered fields are probably references to abandoned corn fields."[7]

The Dispersal of 1649

In 1648, at the beginning of the tragic events that would lead them to abandon Huronia forever, the Wendat told the astonished Jesuits that Quebec was a logical place of refuge.[8] Seeing their nation in peril, in 1650 the Wendat chiefs advised the missionaries that they had decided to abandon Christian Island, where their people had gathered. They delivered a pathetic speech that managed to persuade the missionaries that they must at all costs take the remnants of the Wendat to Quebec, under the protection of the French who themselves had so often been supported by that nation. The chiefs addressed the Jesuits' superior, Father Paul Ragueneau:

> My brother, take courage. You alone can bestow upon us life, if you will strike a daring blow. Choose a place where you may be able to reassemble us, and prevent this dispersion. Cast your eyes toward Quebec and transport thither the remnants of this ruined nation. Do not wait until famine and war have slain the last of us. You bear us in your hands and your heart. More than ten thousand have been snatched away by death. If you delay longer, not one will remain, and then you would know the regret of not having saved those whom you could have withdrawn from

danger and who disclosed to you the means. If you listen to our wishes, we will build a Church under shelter of the fort at Kebec. There, our faith will not die out; and the examples of the Algonquins and of the French will hold us to our duty.[9]

For those "Hurons," Quebec represented the safe, familiar country where they already had ties, the only place where the nation could wrench itself from the threat of death; where the Wendat – accustomed to be at the centre of things, masters of politics and regulators of trade – could hope to go on living as a people, an ally, neither adopted nor immigrants. To these descendants of a nation that had been sacrificed to France and had long guaranteed protection to the French in Huronia, Quebec was the land where some of their ancestors had lived before withdrawing to the shores of Georgian Bay.

The culture of the Stadaconans, even more than the Wendat, bore similarities to that of the surrounding Algonquians. The archaeology of Stadaconan sites shows that agriculture, so essential to the Wendat's social and commercial life, "was not a prime source of subsistence for these people [of the upper St Lawrence valley]" and Pendergast has suggested that "their style of life resembled that of their [more nomadic] Woodland ancestors more than that of the historic Iroquois."[10]

It seems natural that, after their dispersal in the sixteenth century, the Laurentian Nadoueks would have sought refuge among the Wendat who, far more than the Five Nations, shared their commerce-oriented and, to a lesser degree, fishery-oriented culture. Their peaceful disposition as well as their highly developed diplomatic skill would have made the Wendat aware that these refugees would contribute significantly to the commercial and diplomatic expansion they now envisaged, because of the European presence that was an ever-growing menace to the Wendat. The conditions under which these Laurentian peoples were received within the Wendat confederacy would have been most favourable.

The attachment some of the descendants of these refugees retained for their former country and original Stadaconan culture probably played a significant part in the decision made by certain lineages and families after the dispersal of 1649 to flee towards Quebec, the capital of their former country.

The Linguistic Evidence

The Nadouek vocabulary collected by Cartier, mostly at Stadacona in 1535–36, while very limited, has enabled specialists in Amerindian linguistics to determine that the Laurentian language was more closely related to Ontarian Wendat than to any other Nadouek language. "Most linguistic studies have suggested that Laurentian is more closely related to Huron than to the languages of the Five Nations."[11]

The Oral Tradition

Wendat oral tradition indicates that people's awareness that they were sovereign on their own ground and that they had never displaced anyone or encroached upon anyone's territories to use or occupy them. It recalls a constant fraternal harmony in their relations with their neighbours, Montagnais and other Algonquians, and emphasizes that the Wendat have always defended the interests of their Amerindian brothers.

The oral tradition of the neighbouring nations, especially the Montagnais, Algonkin, and Abenaki, invariably concurs with that of Lorette, which recognizes that relations with the Wendat have always been marked by brotherhood and a spirit of mutual assistance. Jean Raphaël, former chief and councillor of the Montagnais nation of Pointe-Bleue, Lac Saint-Jean, and great defender of the Amerindian tradition, expresses the memory of the elders as follows: "Part of the territory [of the Laurentides national park] belonged to the Montagnais of Pointe-Bleue and the other part belonged to the Huron. When those people met, it was a meeting of brothers. There was no dividing them: they could not be divided. In those days, they did meet; an Indian was a brother, you were meeting a brother."[12]

Farther back in time, historian Georges Boiteau recalls the words of another Montagnais, David Basile: "We never have quarrelled with the Hurons, we have always gotten along well with them in the woods, me, my father Malek, and the other old ones before us."[13]

THE WENDAT AFTER 1649

The Seven Nations of Lower Canada

In 1824, Nicolas Vincent Tsaouenhohi (the Eagle), grand chief of the Wendat of Lorette, told the Legislative Assembly of Lower Canada that "two hundred years ago, the Elders of the Seven Nations made an alliance together to live in peace and in common, that is to say that they must eat with the same *micoine* (spoon) from the same bowl: this meant that they all must hunt together [in harmony] on the same lands, to avoid any quarrel among them."[14] His testimony makes reference to an agreement or treaty concluded between the Amerindian nations of Lower Canada around 1650, the year that saw the final dispersal of Huronia and the Wendat's return to Quebec. It is certain that with the arrival came a need to redefine the territorial limits of each of the Seven Nations. In 1824, these were the Iroquois of Oka, Kahnawake, and Saint-Regis; the Abenaki of Bécancour and Odanak; the Wendat of Lorette; and the Algonkin of Trois-Rivières. In 1829, the Wendat of Lorette, keepers of the archives of the nations, possessed among other things a wampum belt which they exhibited in the presence of a government representative, Lieutenant-Colonel Michel-Louis Juchereau Duchesnay, and of chiefs of Native nations, notably of the Algonkin of Trois-Rivières, with the goal of settling a controversy between the nations regarding territorial limits. The Amerindian chiefs acknowledged Chief (of external affairs) Michel Tsiewei's interpretation as being faithful to the ancestral agreements recorded in the wampum, and the matter was settled:

> We, Huron of Lorette, have always been on terms of friendship with our brothers the Algonquin of Trois-Rivières and still remain so.[15] You [addressing Juchereau Duchesnay] tell us of their claims to our hunting limits and I come today to show them they are mistaken and that they are not bound on the East by the Sainte-Anne-de-la-Pérade river as they claim, but by the middle of the Saint-Maurice river. Here is the belt that

shows it. We, or our ancestors for us, have determined with the Algonquin that we shall always hunt together for as long as we do not encounter difficulties, but that if through some misfortune we should encounter any, then our hunting places would be limited as follows: the Huron would be bound in the Northeast by the Saguenay and in the Southwest by the middle of the Saint-Maurice River (with the Algonquin) and by the St. Lawrence River all along until the Saguenay.[16]

Wampum

From the early seventeenth century, because of European iron tools, the nations living on the coast of New England (particularly the Narragansett, Pokanoket, and Massachusetts) were able to increase considerably their production of wampum beads, trade goods much sought-after by both Europeans and Amerindians. From that period, larger and more elaborate wampum "collars" accompanied and sealed most agreements between Amerindians, or between them and the Whites. Elizabeth Tooker notes: "In the seventeenth and eighteenth centuries when wampum was plentiful, it was often woven into belts, and it was in this form that it was usually given to confirm treaties, its design of purple and white beads serving as a mnemonic device to recall the particular treaty it accompanied."[17]

The agreement reached by the Seven Nations "almost two hundred years" before 1829 would coincide both with the time of the exodus from Huronia and with the period when archives, which had earlier existed as collars, took the form of belts that sometimes measured two metres long and fifteen centimetres wide. I believe that the term "collar" in Chief Tsiewei's address was a mistranslation of the word "belt." Even today, in fact, the Wendat realize that their ancestors once possessed wampum or "truth" belts, one of which was the "Kondiaronk's belt of 1701" and another the "Belt of Territories."

The Commercial Genius of the Wendat

In 1650, following their final dispersal from their country in Ontario, the Wendat were already commercially active in their fragile settlement on Île d'Orléans. J.-P. Turcotte, the nineteenth-century

Quebec historian, notes: "In 1650, when a group of Huron were established on Île d'Orléans near Quebec, in order to shield them from Iroquois raids, the first commercial business of this small colony was to go to Tadoussac to trade for furs the corn which they had harvested, which testifies to old customs."[18] This same colony of Wendat on Île d'Orléans was able, during the same period, to make enough beaver-skin blankets to yield for the Jesuits an annual profit of 10,000 *livres tournois* which, according to Trigger, corresponds to 2000 beaver skins. The Wendat were thus repaying the 3000 or so *livres* that had been the yearly cost of maintaining them in Quebec.

The Seigneury of Sillery

In 1651 the Jesuit fathers, after a vast and successful collection of funds among the French aristocracy, acquired for the Wendat and other Christian Indians of Quebec a domain at Sillery (Kamiskda in Algonquian). "In the year 1651," Léon Gérin wrote in 1899, "the king of France had gratified the Christian Indians established in the vicinity of Quebec (the nucleus of whom were the Huron) with a cession of land, covering three miles in width on the St Lawrence by twelve miles in depth."[19] Aside from advancing the cause of Christianization in New France, settling those Amerindians provided the French in Quebec with their surest defence force, and consolidated their commercial base by centralizing the fur trade. Given the destruction of Huronia and the growing Iroquois threat, the Wendat presence was essential to the colony. No effort was spared to attract the greatest possible number of Amerindians to Sillery; in particular, preferential tariffs and prices were instituted for the Christian Indians.

Soon, as the Amerindians at Sillery became less indispensable for French settlement in their country, the Jesuits began wanting to acquire for themselves the property which had been duly allocated to the "civilization of the Hurons and other Indians." In fact, only nine years after "Royal confirmation of the Huron titles," that is in November 1667, the priests acquired about one-third of the Wendat seigneury through a vendor without authorized titles, and then in 1699, unbeknownst to the Wendat proprietors, the remainder of the seigneury. This was a case of fraud committed against the Wendat, and was subsequently recognized as such by all parties concerned, including the king of France who, on 6 May 1702, "confirmed with regret this unjust grant [to the Jesuits]." No one was able to obtain reparations, however, despite a very long Wendat struggle, especially in the nineteenth century. Thus the Wendat lost their greatest chance for a settlement worthy of the ordeals they had endured before acquiring Sillery.

The Wendat in 1763

After yet another dispersal (to Lorette), the Wendat, now deprived of the revenues from leasing their lands, were forced to adapt their culture to the geographical constraints of a territory situated entirely in mountainous country. They turned resolutely towards the forest and their hunting grounds. Their proximity to the city of Quebec, however, allowed them to continue playing an important role in trade and diplomacy. The Wendat war chiefs were generals in the army of Amerindian mercenaries that was so valuable to the French in times of crisis and so highly praised by the missionaries for its zeal at coming to the defence of the French colony. In his report to the British crown on 5 June 1762, General James Murray wrote: "In order to utilize them in times of war with the other Nations, the French Government has always endeavoured, inasmuch as possible, to make the Hurons preserve their ancient customs."[20]

During that period, the Wendat were still playing their traditional role in Amerindian geo-politics. To quote General Murray again: "The most civilized [thus central, and therefore important for the English] of all the Savages in this part of the world are the Hurons established in a small village named Jeune Lorette, situated at three leagues from Quebec ... When comes the hunting seasons, they go into the woods to hunt themselves and to buy the pelts from the Savages who live in far away places."[21] The diplomatic English were well informed about Amerindian geo-politics and dealt with the strategic nations for "trading" purposes. They did so in Montreal, on 5 September 1760, the very day of the capitulation of that city, by signing a separate treaty with the Wendat, which for that people both then and now constitutes recognition of a sovereignty they have never ceded or sold. [22]

In *The Siege of Quebec and the Battle of the Plains of Abraham*, Arthur Doughty wrote: "In the few years immediately preceding the [Seven Years'] war, the history of the Continent could be described in one sentence: the efforts of the English and of the French in order to capture the bulk of Indian trade and thus, to obtain Savage allies in view of the conflict which was imminent. As a general rule, the Indians were entirely neutral. They wished to get the best markets possible for their furs and therefore, were favourable to English traders."[23] The attitude of the victorious British towards the Wendat was inspired by respectful recognition of their special historic status in relation to the other Native nations of Lower Canada, as well as by a need for mutual aid, both commercial and military.

Abandoning the Territories

Government negligence with respect to the survival of Native groups is directly and intimately linked to European belief in the inevitable disappearance of all non-Euroamerican cultures. This conviction is so strong and deeply held that the most draconian and most racist legal and political practices have been used, in all good conscience, to demonstrate its logic or, indeed, its morality. Intimidation by Euroamerican governments, intended to make the Wendat abandon their territories and customs, is consistent with this paternalistic attitude. It is obvious today, however, that this "truth" is not sufficient to guide the Native people on the way of their future. *The Native nations of America are emerging nations*, as their sages always predicted they would be once the Earth-Mother became sufficiently weary of anti-ecological forms of "progress." The Wendat do not want to set themselves outside the modern social process: Natives recognize their responsibility in the search for a solution to the ideological impasse in which Euroamerican civilization finds itself.

In 1824, the Wendat complained to the House of Assembly in Lower Canada that the settlers were mistreating them whenever they had to go onto "their" lands. These Amerindians felt, of course, that only they could claim rights to these lands, while the government was certain there was no need to recognize any rights of a people who were soon to disappear. On 29 January 1824, Grand Chief Vincent talked about:

> the *habitants* who meddle with hunting and fishing and who destroy everything. They set nets for the passenger pigeons [the last bird of that species, once found in "unimaginable" numbers, died in a zoo at the beginning of the twentieth century] and are ready to kill us when we pass the limits of their lands in the woods: they give as their reason that they own those lands in concession and that they are masters on them. Since those Canadian gentlemen have lands to cultivate, let them cultivate them, and leave us our rights to hunt and fish.[24]

Of course the Amerindians' forest land belonged to them less and less. Intimidation continued, mainly through inconsiderate exploitation of the forest's animal and plant resources. Wendat oral tradition indicates that this people has been long and frequently harassed, both in the woods and sometimes "in the village." It recalls the memory of certain Wendat men killed for the furs they possessed or for defying the new owners "despite being warned." Many deaths are still unsolved mysteries.

Still convinced of the Amerindians' imminent disappearance, successive governments have violently (although in good conscience), expelled them from every refuge provided by their land. The "creation" of the Laurentides national park is just one example. Here again is Montagnais chief Jean Raphaël, a man respected as much by the Whites as by his own people. "You know, the national park they've got along the road to Quebec, that used to belong to the Indians, *mon cher monsieur*; there's no getting around that. That land, it belonged to the Huron and to the Montagnais of Pointe-Bleue."[25] Later, he says:

> The terrible shame is that now the Indian has no freedom in the woods ... Today, the Indian makes his home where the forest is nice, let's say for instance a beautiful lake with a fine woods. So then right away the [forest development] company comes along, see, and look what happens: they destroy his place ... There's a lot of them, they've told me about it, some of the young people, they've told me: "I'd like to find

myself a place where I could settle down, a piece of land, a hunting ground, where there'd be some game. The shame of the matter, though, is the companies. They come along and what do they do? Turn it into fields, that's what they do! They take down all the trees, first of all, and after that, well then, all the game disappears needless to say, the game can't stay, it's out of the question.[26]

Restoration of Wendat Rights

I suggest that the historical theories held by governments until our time concerning the future of Natives do not correspond to the new political realities. The regeneration of Native cultures is a fact that no one can seriously deny, one that society at large, which now faces a major ecological crisis, has come to embrace. It is even possible that the strength of Native rights will increase as awareness of the environmental crisis grows.

Thus Wendat rights are very topical now, and the defence of them a responsibility of modern Wendat society. Observing the Wendat nation from its antecedents to the present clearly indicates that its continuing development is of primary importance. Consequently, no effort should be spared to re-establish the Wendat nation's rights and ensure its future growth.

CONCLUSION

I have tried to uncover and explain the foundations of Wendat rights in that nation's traditional territories within Quebec. To do so, I have called on archaeology, ethnohistory, linguistics, Amerindian oral tradition, and ethnographic study of the historical role – mostly commercial and diplomatic – of the Wendat, as well as on Quebec jurisprudence.

I have also laid the basis for a philosophy aimed at integrating Wendat rights into modern sociological discourse on the rights of Native minorities. I believe it is urgent to rouse the Wendat nation from the lethargy in which the many defeats of past centuries have immersed it.

Proponents of modern theses claiming the effective extinction of these unquestionably threatened rights may find some valid objections here. I thank the people who hold such views, because they provide an opportunity to undertake a defence of those rights. When there is no longer anything to defend, there is no more life, and the negation of any form of rights is a loss for all humans. Wendat rights in Quebec are certainly no exception to that rule.

CONCLUSION

This book was written because conventional history has been unable to produce a discourse that respects Amerindians and their perception of themselves and the world, one that would be appropriate to harmonizing society.

Because the problem is as broad and deep as the ocean the Europeans crossed to come here, we have tried to make our method – Amerindian autohistory – a vessel that is as confident of its good fortune as theirs. Our main goal has been to provide modern historical and ethnohistorical (anthropological) science with access to an appropriate knowledge of fundamental Amerindian values. But is there a specific ideological portrait, a specific Amerindian philosophy? Never, across the entire American continent, have there been ideological (political and religious) barriers between different Native groups, and both Amerindians and those who know them well share a deep-rooted cultural kinship, in spite of the physical distances that have often separated them.

We have raised a question that goes back to the arrival of the Europeans in America, namely the inability of non-Native Americans to converse harmoniously with the Native population of this continent, and thus to write about them objectively and scientifically. The proof is the tremendous variety in the historical writing by non-Natives. It has been an essential part of our methodology to examine the true causes of the disastrous contact between the two civilizations. With the help of the new light which recent studies have shed on the history of the depopulation of America, the serious historian will readily understand that epidemic diseases brought from the Old World by Europeans caused the holocaust that destroyed between 80 and 90 per cent of the Amerindian population. For that reason, we have undertaken this study in the context of the microbial fact, which corresponds to the Amerindian mode of thinking: that is, to seek the solution to a problem between humans by cleansing the psyche of negative emotions such as guilt, fear, rancour, and hatred.

Next, we had to expose as myth the belief that the American Native will necessarily disappear, because it strikes us as the main reason for a certain reluctance by historians to incorporate an ethical dimension into their discourse pertaining to Native peoples. We have also insisted on showing the vigour and persistence of Amerindian cultural awareness and, above all, the reasons for its exceptional tenacity. We have taken into account, too, the Americization of the rest of the world since it came into contact with the genius of America. A dehumanized European civilization began to rediscover the reality of human nature and, with the help of its Amerindian teachers, lead the rest of humanity along the path of world socialization. In 1952, the eminent jurist and judge Felix S. Cohen described how the United States had received, in 1744, what was probably the greatest political lesson in known human history. The great Onondaga chief Canasatego had told a council convened by the colonial governors to deal with the Iroquois confederacy: "Our wise forefathers established Union and Amity between the Five Nations. This has made us formidable; this has given us great Weight and Authority with our neighbouring Nations. We are a powerful Confederacy; and by observing the same methods our Wise Forefathers have taken, you too will acquire such strength and power. Therefore, whatever befalls you, never fall out with one another."

"The advice of Canasatego," Cohen continues, "was eagerly taken up by Benjamin Franklin."

"It would be a strange thing, Franklin advised the Albany Congress, if six nations of ignorant savages should be capable of forming a scheme for such an union and be able to execute it in such manner that it has subsisted ages and appears indissoluble, and yet that a like union should be impracticable for ten or a dozen English colonies, to whom it is more necessary and must be more advantageous, and who cannot be supposed to want an equal understanding of their interest."[1]

After briefly enumerating the material gifts of the Amerindian to Europeans (and the world), Cohen describes the transmission of a spiritual legacy:

> If we lost not only the Indian's material gifts, but the gifts of the Indian's spirit as well perhaps we should be just as willing as Europeans have been to accept crusts of bread and royal circuses for the surrender of our freedom. For it is out of a rich Indian democratic tradition that the distinctive political ideals of American life emerged. Universal suffrage for women as well as for men, the pattern of states within a state that we call federalism, the habit of treating chiefs as servants of the people instead of as their masters, the insistence that the community must respect the diversity of men and the diversity of their dreams – all these things were part of the American way of life before Columbus landed.[2]

At the beginning of this work, we explained that the theory of social evolution is a dangerous myth. In 1492, America became the meeting-ground of what were then the two most widely opposed ideologies on earth. Once there was contact with Europeans, Amerindians – because of their circular, non-evolutionist vision – saw the others as humans whose culture was undergoing degeneration and needed to be regenerated, while Europeans, because of their linear and evolutionist vision, saw Amerindians as a backward human type that must at all costs be forced into the European process of evolution and development. At first, both civilizations were sure of their moral superiority. Now, only Amerindian civilization has that certainty.

Modern Amerindians, perhaps even more than those in the past, see the Euroamerican concept of society as mere artifice and illusion. Besides, it is increasingly obvious that the greatest worldwide crisis at this moment is the product of modern human beings who have lost their consciences and ignore the laws of nature. The ecological tragedy that future generations will experience is the harshest punishment the laws of our planet has ever had to impose on humanity.

We now possess enough elements of true knowledge to be able to say that the theory of evolution entails great dangers for the human conscience and spirit, because it lacks solid bases. It is now permissible to think, and urgent to see, that the notion of classifying societies according to their "evolution" has been sheer fantasy on the part of certain civilizations isolated from natural, fundamental needs, which have been busy seeking and perfecting theories to legitimize their cultural imperatives. We know now that these theories have misled human reason and that the latter – if, as we are inclined to believe, it is humanity's fate to struggle for its survival – must proceed to a severe and detailed examination of the underlying values of those "lost" civilizations. A new rationalism enlightened by a will to survive should put an end to the age of evolutionism. Humans have already "evolved" far too much.

If there is to be a positive development of history and of sciences in general ("social" and others), ecology must become the common mother of all sciences; and history, like the social sciences, must consider the ecological dimension as fundamental. The universal goal must be common ecological well-being. Such openness will not be possible, however, until the myth of evolution has been eliminated from human social thought.

In this essay, we have raised the possibility of writing Amerindian history on the basis of values that have not changed through time or, in other words, by making a diachronic comparison of portraits of the Amerindian psyche.

The ethical nature of such an approach to historiography is obvious. It stands in clear opposition to the Euroamerican kind of study of "cultural processes," whose usefulness is not obvious and, indeed, is often debatable for the peoples immediately concerned. Far from bringing benefits to the people whose "cultural conduct is being studied," these scientific games have the unhappy effect of overshadowing their socio-economic condition and of dashing their efforts to restore their historic dignity. Too often, the most laudable efforts to alleviate the painful living conditions of colonized peoples are drowned in a sea of "scientificity."

The autohistorical approach could be illustrated by an example that is diametrically opposed to official history: it is now proper and accepted to see Euroamericans as capable of self-determination. What method could we use to write about them in a respectful manner, given that their written tradition is unreliable and that, besides, we do not know them and are unable to comprehend their feelings and values? The reply of autohistory is that we should let *them* talk, talk about themselves, and thus avoid developing weighty, risky theories.

One example of such a theory is Calvin Martin's 1978 study, *Keepers of the Game*.[3] Here, responsibility for epidemics and thus for the almost total destruction of Amerindian harmony is assigned to the animals. For some obscure reason, they broke the pact of harmony and mutual esteem that had existed from time immemorial and linked them to the Amerindians, and began to spread diseases among them. So it is no longer the Amerindians who are the fierce authors of their self-destruction! No matter: war was declared between them and the animals, and the Amerindians, desperate for new European goods, symbols of luxury and prestige, instantaneously became as bourgeois and "anti-environment" as anyone else. So says Martin. Here again is yet another example of the defeat of the "good Indian," this time described by a neutral scientific analyst as the one who must inevitably lose.

Amerindian knowledge of the laws of ecological balance was just as unconscious as modern industrialized humans' ignorance of these same laws may be. This is no reason to excuse ourselves from objectively studying the nature of these laws, for our benefit or even our survival. Freeing oneself of a sense of guilt by trying to prove that what was destroyed had no particular value is one thing; but reflecting positively about what should be done to check the resulting confusion is something else. Euroamericans need to become responsible, the better to Americize themselves.

EPILOGUE

In the Amerindian's world of plenty, no one is required to believe in the ideology of another. Each person is a vision, a system, a world.

In contrast, when non-Native humans have impoverished their environment to a certain point, quarrels arise to determine who will control the remaining resources, and whom this "victor" will be able to subjugate. In Amerindian eyes, such "nations," who do not really have the right to this title because they exploit their poorest members, may claim technical and material success, but experience social disaster. Who can blame the Amerindian for wanting to preserve a moral sense that is known to be capable of producing a happy and durable social order (in the ecological meaning of the great circle of life)?

Too often, Euroamerican history, because it does not recognize the true impact of knowing the Amerindian moral code, dwells on non-pertinent subjects. Relatively sterile issues (for example, allegations that Natives are only the first immigrants to America, or discussions on the Amerindians' natural ecological sense) obscure questions that are vital for the modern individuals we are, and for the families and societies we form or want to form. Darrell A. Posey is a specialist in Amazonian ethnoecology, particularly that of the Kayapo. He admits that modern society's problems have made it tragically insensitive to the rights of Native peoples throughout the Americas, but says that the greatest tragedy has been the definitive loss of the wisdom, experience, and knowledge of the Native peoples whose cultures have been wiped out:

> Although most Indian societies are already extinct, and those remaining face imminent destruction, there is still time to salvage knowledge about the Amazon [and elsewhere] from surviving indigenous systems. Research must proceed, however, with the utmost urgency and commitment, for with the disappearance of each indigenous group the world loses an accumulated wealth of millennia of human experience and adaptation ...
>
> Following the Kayapo model, we might begin to select as our most important leaders those who will be responsible for the long-term management of natural resources to prevent ecological destruction. At the same time, science must relate its environmental theories in such a way as to show the relevance of ecological balance to each and every individual. Then, and only then, can development proceed with sustainable benefits for the world population as a whole without exploitive resource destruction for the short-term benefit of only a few.[1]

As an international authority on the matter, Posey states his belief in a science of ecology that would draw significantly on Amerindian knowledge: "If the knowledge of indigenous peoples can be integrated with modern technological knowhow, then a new path for ecologically sound development of the Amazon [and other regions] will have been found. Also, if technological civilization begins to realize the practical value of indigenous societies, then Indians can be viewed as intelligent, valuable *people*, rather than just exotic footnotes to history."[2]

The moral code specific to America is so distinctive that the study of it, through history, constitutes a science. Euroamerican specialists, observing the last Native populations who still have a functional social system, now use the term ethnoecology, a science whose goal is an understanding of the biology of environments with the help of Native peoples' ecological knowledge. We see such developments in the social sciences as a sign of Western recognition, late though it may be, of the fundamental value of Native thinking. To amplify and ennoble the significance and application of these new ideas, and to mark both the special character and the obvious interest in a strictly American vision of the world, we shall refer to "Amerology," a new science that would complement the social sciences in their effort to bring their discourse to life and make it available to modern man.

Ethnohistory, despite the great merit of having forged a link between history and anthropology, includes the risk, as Bruce G. Trigger sees it, of perpetuating "an invidious distinction between so-called primitive and complex societies,"[3] and so, in our opinion, of reproducing the method of "divide and conquer." Amerology offers a solution: it removes from both history and the social sciences the notion of a gradation in human societies according to their "evolution," one that underlies all the methodological impasses these disciplines encounter. Amerology is diametrically opposed to the evolutionist notion: it sees all societies as equally human and hence worthy of existing and contributing to the well-being of the whole. Without regard for the conventional order of unilinear evolution, with its fortunate and its condemned, the new science recognizes the diversity of physical constraints (geomorphological, climatic, ecological, and so on) that can influence the *individual* evolution of each human society and thus its estrangement from an ideal harmony with the environment. The science of Amerology aims at offering humanity the understanding of the spiritual essence of a continent whose human civilizations had evolved entirely outside the realm of linear thought characteristic of Euroamerican society and indeed the West as a whole. Globally, America has been and continues to be the place of the circle. Accordingly, Amerology attributes to circular societies (formerly called savage) a spiritual and moral ascendancy over the others, which may be divided into two conventional categories, this time in reverse order: "barbarian" societies (semi-sedentary, agricultural), and civilized (those who have cut themselves off from natural laws).

Societies midway between "savage" and "civilized" have often recognized in the first a proximity to vital spiritual forces and hence the ability to form symbiotic modes of existence or "mixed civilizations." For the civilized, in contrast, these two kinds of societies have always seemed almost equally "backward." In the present circumstances (acute ecological and spiritual crisis), Amerology represents, rather than merely a method and a discipline, a new human awareness and a reflection on the very meaning of the word civilization. This is an innovative concept, one that requires courage, honesty, realism, and intuition on the part of its adherent. Its argument about the characteristics shared by the great majority – perhaps the totality – of Amerindian cultures, requires the unanimous consent both of specialists in Amerindian history and culture, and of Amerindian spiritualists. Because of the growing interest in Amerindian studies, it seems desirable that Amerindian intellectual and spiritual masters should be the leaders of such a science.

To those who still believe that the task of the Euroamerican is to assimilate the Amerindian, we reply in the words of Felix Cohen: "There is still much that we [Euroamericans] can take from the Indian to enrich ourselves without impoverishing the Indian. We have not by any means exhausted the great harvest of Indian inventions and discoveries in agriculture, government, medicine, sport, education and craftsmanship."[4] He concludes: "When we have gathered the last golden grain of knowledge from the harvest of the Indian summer, then we can talk of Americanizing [assimilating] the Indian. Until then, we might do better to concentrate our attention on the real job of the New World, the job of Americanizing [we would say Americizing] the white man."[5]

In concluding this study, I express my confidence that the great circle of relations shall live: and may the one incorporating Amerologists and all those who have an Amerindian soul continue to grow!

APPENDIX

THE INDIAN PROBLEM: A FINAL LOOK

Is it an Indian problem, or a Euroamerican problem? No one knows, has ever known, or will ever know, yet every one must agree that justice has been the missing ingredient in the development of this New World society. Who can truthfully ask why we have been puzzled by an insoluble "Indian problem" throughout these 500 years of contact with the Europeans, while our society still proclaims the exclusive rights of the "discoverer"?

Panamerican jurisprudence is founded on such immortal and venerable principles as:

> All the nations of Europe who have acquired territory on this continent, have asserted in themselves and have recognized in others, the exclusive right of the discoverer to appropriate the lands occupied by the Indians.[1]

Or:

> It was the usage and practice of European nations at that time not to recognize any right to the Native peoples; England, like France, had adopted and applied the customary rule of international law that was generally observed in relations with aboriginal people: the jurisprudence of the time demonstrates that English Common Law in this respect submitted the indigenous populations to English Law and denied them all sovereignty.[2]

These are the bases that support the edifice of the jurisprudence of Canada, Quebec, and all the other colonial states which Europeans have formed in the "discovered" parts of the world. But still no one knows anything about the essence of "the Indian problem."

The territory was emptied by disease, helped along by alcohol and rifles, and the red man's Mother-Earth was taken, used, and mostly abused, her children in their reserves declared spiritually dead in hopeful anticipation. But despite this past, we are still baffled by "the Indian problem."

If a right is to exist, it must be shared; otherwise one of the parties has only the right to disappear. The right of the "discoverer" might have served as an elegant justification until recent times, so long as the Dark Ages still existed. But to persist in claiming that the "discoverer" acquired exclusive rights to the lands and peoples "discovered," and to base legal systems on such axioms while hoping to solve "the Indian problem," strikes me as tantamount to thinking that the best way to reach an enlightened decision is by immersing oneself in the dark.

What is most regrettable about this collective frame of mind is that the vast majority of people have been taken in. In fact, if we examine the question honestly, none of us, Amerindian or not, comes across as dazzlingly intelligent. Self-esteem is the source of all social virtues, and "the Indian problem" is unquestionably one of the main reasons for the loss of individual and collective pride among the inhabitants of "discovered" lands. No matter how the acquisition is made, there is a price to pay for obtaining anything. In the present case, the price all of us are still paying is well beyond our human means. The disastrous way we view and treat the environment is directly linked with our conception of justice and property rights. In 1855, Chief Seattle of the Squamish nation warned the Euroamerican nations: "Whatever befalls the Earth befalls the children of the Earth … All things are connected, like the blood which unites one family. Continue to contaminate your bed and you will one day suffocate in your own waste."

It is urgent that the Euroamerican notion of rights of occupation – indeed, the very concept of discovery – be abandoned. Why, I ask, following my ancestors' natural philosophy, do descendants of the European invaders deny the original inhabitants any right to the soil in which they are so deeply rooted? If an adult orphan should claim possession of my mother and take her by force, what would I think? What would *he* or *she* think? We would both look like fools. But could I stop my mother from taking on as an adoptive child someone who feels the need of such a relationship? My ancestors never tried to prevent such ties between their Mother-Earth and the newcomers; on the contrary, they always rejoiced at the prospect of welcoming new members into their families and naturalizing them, that is, sharing all their rights with them. In my opinion, Amerindians' attitude and vision have been gravely misjudged from the beginning: the Native peoples were perfectly capable of respecting and accepting people from other cultures; healthy attitudes towards other societies often existed, but they were systematically discouraged, even suppressed, by the European élites. "The Indian problem" we have today is an ideological legacy from colonial times. Moreover, I firmly believe that history is the normal and natural unfolding of human existence; no one, then, should be blamed or praised for the way in which events occur. However, if humans can only go forward, they have both the responsibility and the power continually and rationally to revise their goals and their philosophy, so as to continue a happy journey on the marvellous planet that is Earth.

While I do not want to make a separate case for the Native nations who have signed treaties, I wish to note a singularly obscure type of land-rights acquisition. The Royal Proclamation of 1763 stipulated that the Amerindian land title had been erased by the conquest of the occupied territories, whether by France or England. First, there is no question that the territories in question were never "conquered" in the European sense of the term. As we have stated earlier, the European notion that nation-states had the moral obligation and hence the right to dispossess savage peoples of their lands in order to bring them under civilized law had, as its Amerindian counterpart, the idea that Native people had an obligation to share their continent with the newcomers. That implies, at least to Amerindians, that even if there was a conquest, the use of force can never give a nation-state the right to oppress conquered peoples. Of course, this view runs counter to the various concepts used to justify theories of conquest and, consequently, to the legal system that currently exists in Canada and in all the other "discovered" parts of the world.

As William J. Eccles, professor of Canadian history at the University of Toronto, observes in describing the Europeans' unjust acquisition of territorial rights: "Such (!) were the means whereby sovereignty and title to the lands of the Indians were eventually acquired. They *certainly* were not acquired by virtue of France having ceded a nonexistent title to the British Crown in 1763."[3]

Is there anyone who knows how "the Indian problem" came to be? We have always been told that a solution will soon be found, but it has proved more difficult than anyone expected. In fact, we are now certain that Amerindian sovereignty is a growing phenomenon. Is it not then time to re-examine both the historical and ideological reality of the entire question?

In May 1982 – in an incident alluded to earlier – four members of the Wendat nation (including myself) and one member of the Anishnabe nation were arrested by Quebec Wildlife Conservation officers while performing their annual rites of purification and thanksgiving. This occurred within the limits of a provincial park whose creation, in 1906, had entailed the unconditional eviction of the Montagnais and Wendat occupants; these people were "legally" dispossessed of their territories by virtue of the sacrosanct Royal Proclamation of 1763. As former occupants, the Wendat had been allowed to exercise certain very poorly defined rights, including the right to off-season fishing and hunting. In 1976, however, the government put an end to the dubious status of these Amerindians in relation to the park.

In accordance with traditional recognition of their relationship with the rest of creation and their duty to protect it, these Natives, along with their wives and children, were accused of having "mutilated the forest": their fasting lodges had been made from pliable young saplings (an offering and prayer always accompany the act of taking these). Yet all around are thousands of square kilometres of decimated, even irreversibly ravaged forest. "The Indian problem" is sometimes disconcertingly subtle: mutilation of trees by traditional Amerindians is denounced, while exploitation by forest-development companies is tolerated. In 1987, the Quebec Court of Appeal overturned the guilty verdict handed down against the defendants by two successive Quebec courts. Quebec then brought the case before the Supreme Court of Canada, which in May 1990 gave a unanimous verdict in favour of the defendants.

"The Indian problem" has universal dimensions: there is nothing selfish about the Amerindian's struggle. Since European contact, the aboriginal nations of America – Chief Seattle's words and the teachings of numerous Amerindian sages testify to this – have acknowledged their responsibility towards their white brethren. The latter were obviously disoriented in relation to the natural laws; a large portion of humanity was thus led to see only temporary and selective material success, with no concern for permanent and general spiritual impoverishment. The misfortunes of my people strike me as relative compared with the tragic existence of my white brothers and sisters; in fact, through no fault of theirs, the vicissitudes of their own destiny caused them long ago to lose the sense of human existence and nature. Because of their uniquely keen perception of the natural order, Amerindians have felt from their first meeting with Europeans that these people were coming here out of a pressing need to relearn their own relationship with other humans and the rest of creation. Even if the first Americans foresaw that the coming of the Europeans would produce a shock both overwhelming and catastrophic for them and for the land, they could also imagine what would come after: Whites, horrified by the socio-ecological mess they had made of the continent, would one day turn to Native people and ask their help in re-establishing order, and thus in finding a solution to "the Indian problem."

I for one have never been satisfied with the image of myself, of my people, or of anyone else in the overall picture. As a matter of fact, no one in it seems very highly developed. Like what I believe to be an ever-growing majority of Americans (in the broad sense of inhabitants of the Americas), I think it's time that we address the facts and not just the ideology. We know that, to date, we have never been told the truth, and we need to hear the truth. We know about past injustices and we require that justice be done. It seems to me that we should put the old "justice system" to rest, get rid of the stupid, brutal "right of the discoverer," and shelve the Royal Proclamation and other such absurd colonial contrivances. Finally, let us make room for the first nations of America around the conference table of the United Nations, let us recognize their rights and titles to the whole of the continent, and let us ask the nations of immigrants that have formed here to make the case for their territorial occupation to those who have been the guardians of America from time immemorial. Let them express their needs in terms of their own cultures and their social and technological projects, so that rational solutions can be found that will satisfy, reassure, and pacify all parties concerned. That is the way to genuine and enduring material and spiritual enrichment, and thus to world peace.

This process of world pacification has been slowly evolving since the "discovery" of America. Let's allow this evolution to continue, for the benefit and well-being of humankind. And then let's forget about "the Indian problem!"

NOTES

INTRODUCTION

1 William Robertson, *The History of America* (London: Printed for W. Strahan, T. Cadell, and J. Balfour), 4:282.

CHAPTER ONE

1 Henry F. Dobyns, "Estimating Aboriginal American Populations. An Appraisal of Techniques with a New Hemispheric Estimate," *Current Anthropology* 5, no. 4 (1966): 414–15.

2 Ibid., 412–14.

3 Emmanuel Le Roy-Ladurie, *Le Territoire de l'historien* (Paris: Gallimard 1978), first part: "Un concept: l'unification microbienne du monde," 86.

4 Woodrow Borah, "America as a Model. The Demographic Impact of European Expansion upon the Non-European World," cited in Le Roy-Ladurie, *Le Territoire de l'historien*, 96.

5 Remarks by John Mohawk, Seneca historian and professor at the University of Buffalo, New York, during a conference on Iroquois communications, 11–12 April 1985, at the Native American Center for the Living Arts, Niagara Falls, New York. Author's personal files.

6 François Du Creux, in James B. Conacher, ed., *The History of Can-*

ada or New France, 2 vols. (New York: Greenwood Press 1969), 2:700.

7 Reuben Gold Thwaites, ed., *The Jesuits' Relations and Allied Documents, 1610–1791*, 73 vols. (New York: Pageant Books 1959), 35:198, 204.

8 Ibid., 19:93.

9 Red Rising Sun of the Klamath Nation, Oregon, "The Real American Dream," *Akwesasne Notes*, Spring 1976, 36.

CHAPTER TWO

1 Hehaka Sapa (Black Elk), *Les rites secrets des Indiens sioux*, texts collected and annotated by Joseph Epes Brown (Paris: Payot 1975), 26.

2 Remarks by Peter Ochees, Anishnabe (Ojibwa) holy man, during a time devoted to traditional rites. Author's personal files (translated by Eddie Bellerose, Cree sage and director of Four Skies Consulting, Edmonton, Alberta).

3 Henry F. Dobyns, *Their Number Become Thinned. Native American Population Dynamics in Eastern North America* (Knoxville, University of Tennessee Press 1983), 33–146.

4 Basil H. Johnston, "The Vision," *Tawow* 6, no. 1 (1978): 14–15.

5 Daniel Garrison Brinton, *The Myths of the New World. A Treatise on the Symbolism and Mythology of the Red Race of America* (New York, Leopold and Holt 1868), 20.

6 Ibid, 6.

7 Pierre Clastres, *La société contre l'État* (Paris, Éditions de Minuit 1974), 28.

8 Brinton, *The Myths of the New World, 21.*

9 Reference to an article by Felix S. Cohen, "Americanizing the White Man," *The American Scholar* 20, no. 2 (1952): 177–90.

10 Johann Jakob Bachofen, *Du règne de la mère au patriarcat* (Paris, Ed. de l'Aire 1983), 43.

11 Shepard Krech III, "Disease, Starvation and Social Organization of the Northern Athapascan," *American Ethnologist* 5, no. 4 (1978): 722.

12 Johann Jakob Bachofen, *Le droit de la mère dans l'Antiquité* [*Das Mutterrecht*] (Paris, Groupe français d'études féministes 1903), 66–7.

13 Ibid., 36, preface.

14 Joseph François Lafitau, *Customs of the American Indians Compared with the Customs of Primitive Times* (translated from: *Moeurs des Sauvages amériquains, comparés aux moeurs des premiers temps*, translated

and edited by William N. Fenton and Elizabeth L. Moore, 2 vols. (Toronto: The Champlain Society 1974), 1:69.

15 Ibid., 1:343–4.

16 Bachofen, *Le droit de la mère dans l'Antiquité*, 37–8.

17 Judith K. Brown, "Economic Organization and the Position of Women among the Iroquois," *Ethnohistory* 17, no. 4 (1970): 164.

18 Bachofen, *Le droit de la mère dans l'Antiquité*, 64–5.

19 Georgina Tobac (Athabascan), North West Territory, speaking in a film by René Fumoleau, *Dene Nation* (National Film Board of Canada 1979).

CHAPTER 3

1 Bruce G. Trigger, *The Children of Aataentsic. A History of the Huron People to 1660* (Montreal and London: McGill-Queen's University Press 1976), 6.

2 Donald B. Smith, *Le "Sauvage" pendant la période héroïque de la Nouvelle-France*, Collection "Cultures Amérindiennes," Cahiers du Québec (Montreal: Hurtubise/HMH 1974), 133. My emphasis.

3 Ben Kroup, anthropologist, interview in *Turtle Quarterly*, first issue, 1986, 14–16.

4 Rémi Savard, *Destins d'Amérique. Les autochthones et nous* (Montreal: Ed. de l'Hexagone 1979), 15.

5 Remarks by Oren Lyons, traditional chief and orator of the Onondaga nation at Onondaga, New York, during a conference on Iroquois communications, 11 and 12 April 1985, at the Native American Center for the Living Arts, Niagara Falls, New York. Author's personal files.

6 Remarks by Peter Ochees, Anishnabe (Ojibwa) holy man, during a time devoted to traditional rites. Author's personal files (translated by Eddie Bellerose, Cree sage and director of Four Skies Consulting, Edmonton, Alberta).

7 T.C. McLuhan, *Touch the Earth* (New York: Outerbridge & Lazard 1971), 18.

8 Alexander Henry, in James Bain, ed., *Travels and Adventures in Canada and the Indian Territories* (Saint-Clair Shores, Michigan: Scholarly Press 1972), 139.

9 Calvin Martin, "The Metaphysics of Writing Indian-White History," *Ethnohistory* 26, no. 2 (1979): 155.

10 Ibid., 156.

11 Ibid., 158.
12 McLuhan, *Touch the Earth*, 6.
13 Denys Delâge, *Le pays renversé. Amérindiens et Européens en Amérique du Nord-Est, 1600–1664* (Montreal: Boréal Express 1985), 76–7.
14 Pierre Clastres, *La société contre l'Etat* (Paris: Ed. de Minuit 1974), 22.
15 Reuben Gold Thwaites, ed., *The Jesuits' Relations and Allied Documents, 1610–1791*, 73 vols. (New York: Pageant Books 1959), 32:283.
16 Marshall D. Sahlins, *Stone Age Economics* (Chicago and New York, Aldine-Asherton 1972), 182.
17 Peter Wraxall, in Charles H. McIlwain, ed., *An Abridgement of the Indians Affairs Contained in Four Folio Volumes, Transacted in the Colony of New York from the Year 1678 to the Year 1751* (Cambridge, Harvard University Press), "Harvard Historical Studies" coll., vol. 21 (1915): 195.
18 Pierre F.X. de Charlevoix, *Histoire et description générale de la Nouvelle-France*, cited in Maurice Roelens, ed., *Dialogues avec un Sauvage* (Montreal, Ed. Leméac 1974), 111–12n.
19 National Archives of Canada, Series C–11–A, vol. VII, Denonville to Colbert, Marquis de Seignelay, 13 November 1685, 46–7.
20 Chrestien LeClercq, *Nouvelles relations de la Gaspésie (1691)*, translated and edited by W.F. Ganong (Toronto: The Champlain Society 1910), 108.
21 Anonymous (Inuit author from Happy Valley, Labrador), "Eskimo Way of Life Today," unpublished documents, Ottawa-Hull, Department of Indian and Northern Affairs, (b).
22 McLuhan, *Touch the Earth*, 63.
23 Remarks by Abraham Burnstick, Cree-Assiniboine (Stoney) holy man.
24 McLuhan, *Touch the Earth*, 170–1.
25 Jean-François Graugnard and others, ed., *Voix indiennes. Le message des Indiens d'Amérique au monde occidental* (Paris: Les Formes du secret 1979), 115.
26 Ibid., 125–7.
27 Remarks by Oren Lyons.
28 Remarks by John Mohawk, Seneca historian and professor at the University of Buffalo, New York, during a conference on Iroquois communications, 11–12 April 1985, at the Native American Center for the Living Arts, Niagara Falls, New York. Author's personal files.

29 Ibid.

30 Interview with Jean Raphaël (aged seventy-seven), sage and former chief of the Montagnais of Mashteuiatsh (Pointe Bleue), at Lac à Jim, Lac Saint-Jean, 15 March 1985. Author's personal files.

31 Speech by George Clutesi, then aged eighty-one and since deceased, painter, writer, actor, sage of the Tseshaht nation, Vancouver Island, at Port Alberni, 27 April 1985. Author's personal files.

32 Armand Collard, poet and thinker of the Montagnais nation at Betsiamites, Quebec, "Barefoot on the Massacred Earth," unpublished poem, 1985. Author's personal files.

33 Willie Lawrence Dunn, author-composer from the Micmac nation, Restigouche, Quebec, producer of the film *Crowfoot*, 1967; song entitled "O Canada."

34 Dr Eléonore Sioui Jikonsaseh, *Andatha*, poems (Val d'Or, Editions Hyperborée, Collection "Bribes d'univers," 1985), 24.

35 Taki Ongoy, Argentinian Native musical group directed by Victor Heredia; song entitled "Taki Ongoy," 1986. Private collection of Native music of the Americas. (Freely translated)

36 *Consejo mundial de pueblos indigenas [World Council of Indigenous Peoples]*, Ottawa, Bulletin no. 1 (1988): 7.

37 Interview with Professor Roberto Cardoso de Oliveira, *Revista de Actualidade Indigena*, Brasilia 3, no. 18 (September-October 1979): 51–2.

38 "Amazonia: a briga pelo verde [Amazonia: The Battle for the Forest], *Afinal*, Manaus, Brazil, no. 236 (7 March 1989): 78. (Translated from the Portuguese by Georges Sioui.) The tragedies mentioned occurred in the 1970s, when Native societies in Brazil suffered substantial depopulation and severe social breakdown as a direct consequence of the installation of huge hydroelectric projects – all of which have been described as failures on environmental, sociological, and technological grounds.

39 Bruce G. Trigger, "Archaeology and the Future," Distinguished Lectures, Montreal, McGill University, Faculty of Arts, 11 November 1986, 37.

40 A fuller treatment of this and a host of other aspects of Wendat and Iroquois history and culture is part of the subject of my forthcoming book, *La Civilisation Wendate*, to be published by Les Presses de l'Université Laval in 1992.

CHAPTER 4

1 Karl H. Schlesier, "Epidemics and Indian Middlemen. Rethinking the Wars of the Iroquois," *Ethnohistory* 23, no. 2 (1976): 131.
2 Ibid., 29.
3 Interview with Louis Hall Karaniaktajeh (aged sixty-eight), painter and writer of the Mohawk nation of Kahnawake, at Kahnawake, 5 July 1985. Author's personal files.
4 James A. Tuck, "Northern Iroquoian Prehistory," in Bruce G. Trigger, ed., *Handbook of North American Indians* 15 (Northeast) (Washington: Smithsonian Institution 1978), 324.
5 See section on "The Archaeological Evidence" in Chapter 6.
6 Elizabeth Tooker, "The League of the Iroquois. Its History, Politics and Ritual," in Trigger, *Handbook of North American Indians*, 15:419–22.
7 John Napoleon Brinton Hewitt, cited in ibid., 15:421–2.
8 William Douw Lightall, *Hochelagans and Mohawks* (Ottawa: J. Hope and Sons 1899), 208–9.
9 Henry F. Dobyns, *Their Number Become Thinned. Native American Population Dynamics in Eastern North America* (Knoxville: University of Tennessee Press 1983), 314–21.
10 Bruce G. Trigger, *The Children of Aataentsic. A History of the Huron People to 1660*, cited in John A. Dickinson, "Annaotaha et Dollard vus de l'autre côté de la palissade," *Revue d'histoire de l'Amérique française* 35, no. 2 (1981): 171.
11 Ibid., 177–8.
12 Reuben Gold Thwaites, ed., *The Jesuits' Relations and Allied Documents, 1610–1791*, 73 vols. (New York: Pageant Books 1959) 15:171.
13 Schlesier, cited in ibid., 25:105, 109.
14 Ibid., 141.
15 William N. Fenton, "Northern Iroquoian Culture Patterns," in Trigger, *Handbook of North American Indians*, 15:315.
16 Remarks by John Mohawk, Seneca historian and professor at the University of Buffalo, New York, during a conference on Iroquois communications, 11–12 April 1985, at the Native American Center for the Living Arts, Niagara Falls, New York. Author's personal files.
17 Joseph-François Lafitau, *Moeurs des Sauvages américains comparées aux*

moeurs des premiers temps, edited, introduced, and annotated by Edna Hindie Lemay, 2 vols. (Paris: Maspéro 1983) 2:88.

18 Ibid., 2:83.

19 Ibid., 1:99.

20 Ibid., 2:12.

21 Ibid., 2:6 (my emphasis).

22 Ibid., 2:6–7.

23 Ibid., 2:27.

24 Ibid., 1:80.

25 Ibid., 2:13.

26 Bartolomé de las Casas, *Brevisima Relacion de la Destruccion de las Indias* (Santiago de Chili: Editorial Nascimiento 1972), 30. (Translated from the Spanish by Georges Sioui.)

27 Lafitau, *Moeurs des Sauvages américains*, vol. 2.

28 Université de Montréal historian John A. Dickinson has carried out a critical study of the "great number" of French victims of the Iroquois during this period. See Dickinson, "La guerre iroquoise et la mortalité en Nouvelle-France, 1608–1666," *Revue d'histoire de l'Amérique française* 36, no. 1 (June 1982): 31–47.

29 Lafitau, *Moeurs des Sauvages américains*, vol. 2.

30 Ibid., vol. 2.

31 Ibid., vol. 2.

32 Ibid., 2:111.

33 Joseph Le Caron, "Plainte de la Nouvelle-France dite Canada à la France sa germaine" (factum) (Paris 1626).

34 Lafitau, *Moeurs des Sauvages américains*, 2:88.

35 Ibid., 2:95.

36 Ibid., 2:91.

37 Ibid., 2:98.

38 Donald H. Frame, ed., *Montaigne's Essays and Selected Writings*, cited in Cornelius J. Jaenen, *Friend and Foe* (Toronto: McClelland and Stewart 1973), 122.

39 Lafitau, *Moeurs des Sauvages américains*, 2:31.

40 Ibid., 1:234.

41 Ibid., 1:232.

42 Ibid., 1:157.

43 Ibid., 1:145.

44 Ibid., 1:146.

45 Ibid., 1:23.
46 Ibid., 1:182.
47 Ibid., 2:151–2.
48 Robert E. Berkhofer, Jr., "The Political Context of a New Indian History," *Pacific Historical Review* 40, no. 3 (1971): 358.
49 Remarks by Doug George, historian and journalist of the Mohawk nation of Akwesasane (Quebec, Ontario, and New York), during a conference on Iroquois communications, 11–12 April 1985, at the Native American Center for the Living Arts, Niagara Falls, New York. Author's personal files.
50 Ibid.
51 Ibid.
52 Ibid.

CHAPTER 5

1 Jacques Collin, presentation, chronology, and notes, *Louis-Armand de Lom d'Arce, baron de Lahontan*, oeuvre I: *Nouveaux voyages en Amérique septentrionale* (Montreal: L'Hexagone et Minerve 1983), 43.
2 Donald H. Frame, ed., *Montaigne's Essays and Selected Writings*, cited in Cornelius J. Jaenen, *Friend and Foe* (Toronto: McClelland and Stewart 1973), 28.
3 Réal Ouellet, texts presented and annotated by, *Sur Lahontan* (Quebec: L'Hêtrière 1983 [pre-publication]), 102–3.
4 Ibid., 7.
5 Ibid., 7.
6 Ibid., 50.
7 Louis-Armand de Lom d'Arce de Lahontan, *Mémoires de l'Amérique septentrionale* (La Haye, Lhonoré, original 1709 edition), preface, 4–5.
8 Ouellet, *Sur Lahontan*, 47.
9 Ibid., 47–8.
10 Ibid., 48. While acknowledging the morality in Confucian teachings, the Jesuits did not allow an equal place in heaven to Christian Chinese who professed reverence for basic Confucian philosophical tradition.
11 Ibid., 51.
12 Ibid.
13 Ibid., 54.

14 Ibid.
15 Ibid., 105.
16 Pierre F.X. de Charlevoix, *Histoire et description générale de la Nouvelle-France*, cited in Maurice Roelens, *Dialogues avec un Sauvage* (Montreal: Leméac 1974), 45n.18.
17 J.-Edmond Roy, *Le baron de Lahontan* (Montreal: Ed. Elysée 1974), 90.
18 Ibid., 48.
19 Preface to the 1703 edition of *Dialogues avec un Sauvage*, cited in Roelens, *Dialogues avec un Sauvage*, 43.
20 Roy, *Le baron de Lahontan*, 93.
21 Charlevoix, *Histoire*, cited in Roelens, *Dialogues avec un Sauvage*, 45.
22 Roelens, *Dialogues avec un Sauvage*, 116.
23 Métis historian Olive Patricia Dickason, in *The Myth of the Savage and the Beginnings of French Colonialism in the Americas* (University of Alberta Press 1984), provides a revealing analysis of Amerindian perceptions of European customs and social traits, particularly in Chapter 10: "Amerindians in Europe," 203–30.
24 Ibid., 199.
25 Ibid., 199.
26 Eddie Bellerose, Cree sage and director of Four Skies Consulting, Edmonton, Alberta, sums up with this maxim the Amerindian idea of faith.
27 Ouellet, *Sur Lahontan*, 80–1. My emphasis.
28 Louis Hall Karaniaktajeh, *Indian Survival Crisis Bulletin 10* (Kahnawake, Quebec), 1.
29 Roy, *Le baron de Lahontan*, 207.
30 Ibid.
31 Ibid., 238.
32 Ibid., 238–9.
33 Basnage de Beauval, *Histoire des ouvrages des savans*, cited in Ouellet, *Sur Lahontan*, 24–5.
34 Ibid., 111–12.
35 Ibid., 113. My emphasis.
36 Ibid., 116.
37 Ibid., 117–18.
38 Roy, *Le baron de Lahontan*, 271.
39 Roelens, *Dialogues avec un Sauvage*, 124.
40 Ibid., 125.

41 Ibid., 140.
42 Ibid., 125.
43 Ibid., 129–30. My emphasis.
44 Ibid., 131.
45 Ibid., 132.
46 Ibid., 132–3.
47 Ibid., 134.
48 Ibid., 139.
49 Ibid., 138.
50 Ibid.
51 Jacques Bernard, *Nouvelles de la république des lettres,* cited in Ouellet, *Sur Lahontan,* 65–6.
52 Roelens, *Dialogues avec un Sauvage,* 143–4.
53 Ibid., 148.
54 Ibid., 149.
55 Ibid.
56 Lom d'Arce de Lahontan, *Memoires,* 140.
57 Roelens, *Dialogues avec un Sauvage,* 158.
58 Ibid.
59 Ibid., 156.
60 Ibid., 156–7. Observers of earlier periods have, of course, universally noted that women did not cover their breasts during the warmer times of the year.
61 Ibid., 126.
62 Ibid., 163.
63 Ibid.
64 David M. Hayne, ed., "Lom d'Arce de Lahontan, Louis-Armand de," *Dictionary of Canadian Biography,* 13 vols. to date, vol. 2 (Toronto: University of Toronto Press 1969), 444.
65 Roy, 117.
66 Ouellet, 50–1.
67 Ibid., 7.
68 Ibid., 106–8.
69 Lom d'Arce de Lahontan, *Memoires,* 7.

CHAPTER 6

1 The St Lawrence Iroquoians are renamed the Laurentian Nadoueks in my forthcoming book, *La Civilisation Wendate.*
2 James A. Tuck, "Northern Iroquoian Prehistory," in Bruce G. Trig-

ger, ed. *Handbook of North American Indians*, vol. 15 (Northeast), (Washington: Smithsonian Institution 1978), 324.

3 Bruce G. Trigger, "Early Iroquoian Contacts with Europeans," in ibid., 344.

4 Gabriel Sagard-Théodat, *Le grand voyage au pays des Hurons*, presented by Marcel Trudel (Montreal: Hurtubise HMH 1976), introduction, xliii-xliv.

5 Bruce G. Trigger, "The Historic Location of the Hurons," *Ontario History* 44, no. 2 (1962): 144.

6 William N. Fenton, "Northern Iroquoian Culture Patterns," in Trigger, *Handbook of North American Indians*, 15:302.

7 Conrad E. Heidenreich, "Huron," in ibid., 369.

8 Reuben Gold Thwaites, ed., *The Jesuits' Relations and Allied Documents, 1610–1791*, 73 vols. (New York: Pageant Books 1959), vol. 34:222.

9 Ibid., 35:192–4.

10 Bruce G. Trigger, "Archaeological and Other Evidence. A Fresh Look at the Laurentian Iroquois," *American Antiquity* 33, no. 4 (1968): 436.

11 Ibid.

12 Interview with Jean Raphaël, (aged seventy-seven), sage and former chief of the Montagnais of Mashteuiatsh (Pointe Bleue), at Lac à Jim, Lac Saint-Jean, 15 March 1985. Author's personal files.

13 Georges Boiteau, "Les chasseurs hurons de Lorette," MA thesis, Université Laval, 1954, 87.

14 Nicolas Vincent Tsaouenhohi, civilian grand chief of the Wendat of Wendake (Lorette), 1810–1844; minutes of the Lower Canada Chamber of Assembly, 29 January 1824.

15 Additional proof of the "prehistoricity" of harmonious relations between the ancestors of the Algonquins and the Wendat, and of the territorial agreement between the two groups, is provided in the report of the exploration of the Beaumier archaeological site, located three kilometres from the mouth of the Saint-Maurice, on the east bank of the river. Excavation has shown that "during that period (800 to 1500 A.D.), the middle valley of the St. Lawrence constituted a centre of cultural development the end of which was probably associated with the St Lawrence Iroquoians met by Jacques Cartier during the 16th century." And comparing the Beaumier site with the Dawson site (Montreal island) and the Pointe-au-Buisson site, the report suggests that "the people who occupied

these three sites maintained frequent contacts, probably because they shared the same culture, in which a regional division between Hochelaga and Stadacona is beginning to be noted." Roger Marois, *Le gisement Beaumier. Essai sur l'évolution des décors de céramique* (Ottawa: Musée national de l'Homme, coll. "Mercure"), 7 (1978): 106–7. The study of several other St Lawrence valley sites has since confirmed these hypotheses. (See in particular the work by Normand Clermont, Claude Chapdelaine, and Georges Barré, *Le site iroquoien de Lanoraie. Témoignage d'une maison-longue.* (Montreal: Recherches amérindiennes au Québec 1983.)

16 Boiteau, "Les chasseurs hurons de Lorette," 12.

17 Elizabeth Tooker, "The League of the Iroquois. Its History, Politics and Ritual," in Trigger, *Handbook of North American Indians*, 15:423.

18 Louis-Philippe Turcotte, *Histoire de l'île d'Orléans*, Atelier typographique du *Canadien*, 1867, 20.

19 Léon Gérin, "The Hurons of Lorette" (Ottawa: *Transactions of the Ottawa Literary and Scientific Society* 1900), no. 2, 83.

20 Murray, General James. "Report to His Britannick Majesty, June 5th, 1762," *Canadian Archives: Documents Relating to the Constitutional History of Canada*. Sessional Papers no. 18, edited by Adam Short and Arthur Doughty (Ottawa 1907), 55.

21 Ibid. My emphasis.

22 In May 1990, the Wendat of Wendake (Quebec) won a landmark case (the *Sioui* case) involving territorial and religious rights when the Supreme Court of Canada recognized this 1760 agreement as a treaty (see appendix).

23 A. Doughty, in collaboration with G.W. Parmelee, *The Siege of Quebec and the Battle of the Plains of Abraham*, 6 vols. (Quebec, Dussault et Proulx 1901), 2:196.

24 Nicolas Vincent Tsaouenhohi, minutes of the Lower Canada Chamber of Assembly, 29 January 1824.

25 Interview with Jean Raphaël.

26 Ibid.

CONCLUSION

1 Felix S. Cohen, "Americanizing the White Man," *The American Scholar* 20, no. 2 (1952): 183–4.

2 Ibid., 179–80.

3 Calvin Martin, *Keepers of the Game. Indian-Animal Relationships and the Fur Trade* (Berkeley and Los Angeles: University of California Press 1978).

EPILOGUE

1 Darrell A. Posey, "Indigenous Ecological Knowledge and Development of the Amazon," in Emilio Moran, ed., *The Dilemma of Amazonian Development* (Boulder: Westview Press 1984), 248–9.

2 Ibid., 225.

3 Bruce G. Trigger, *The Children of Aataentsic. A History of the Huron People to 1660* (Montreal and London: McGill-Queen's University Press 1976), 12.

4 Felix S. Cohen, "Americanizing the White Man," *The American Scholar*, 20, no. 2 (1952): 190.

5 Ibid., 191.

APPENDIX

1 *Johnson* v. *McIntosh*, Supreme Court of the United States, 1883.

2 *James Bay Development Corporation* v. *Chief Robert Kanatewat*, 1975, Quebec Court of Appeal.

3 William J. Eccles, "Franco-Indian Relations 1534–1763," July 1984, 39. Author's personal files.